PRAISE F[

"[This] book is beyond s
delightful, and profound."
— **Christiane Northrup, M.D.,** best-selling author of
Women's Bodies, Women's Wisdom

"I absolutely love this book. Pam has combined a writing style as
funny as Ellen DeGeneres with a wisdom as deep and profound
as Deepak Chopra's to deliver a powerful message and a set of
experiments that will prove to you beyond a doubt that our
thoughts really do create our reality."
— **Jack Canfield,** co-creator of the *New York Times* best-selling
Chicken Soup for the Soul® series and *The Success Principles*

"I figure if a 53-year-old Midwestern, skeptical, tough-talking radio
host found this perhaps the most insightful and on-target book with
regard to 'how it works,' then the bestseller list cannot be far behind.
[Pam's] journey . . . message and honesty and humor about
the human condition are nothing short of profound."
— **John St. Augustine,** former producer for *Oprah and Friends*
and author of *Every Moment Matters*

"I drank in this book like a tall lemonade on a hot day. I kept
highlighting, and writing things in the margins like 'Yes!' This is a truly
glorious book: in-your-face and young and fun, yet wise in a very deep
and satisfying way. Pam Grout doesn't pull any punches: you may agree
with her take on spirituality or you may not, but I can't believe anyone
could read this book and not feel surer that there's a positive purpose
to all this. That we're loved. That we have important work to do."
— **Victoria Moran,** life coach and author of ten books, including
Creating a Charmed Life and *Lit from Within*

"This book is a refreshing guide to practical mysticism. I love that it
doesn't ask me to throw out reason. Instead, I get to satisfy the skeptic
in me by trying out these simple experiments and looking at the
results for myself. And guess what? They work!"
— **Dr. Dave Smiley,** creator of *The Inner Weigh*®, a film about
spirituality, the mind, and physical transformation

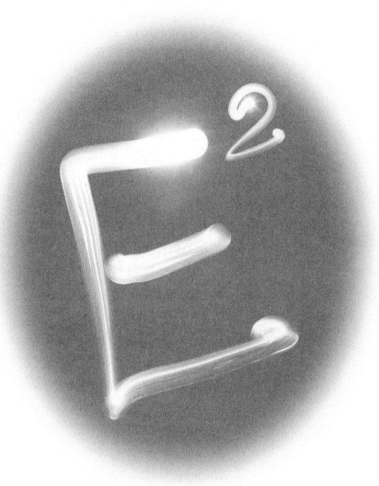

Hay House Titles of Related Interest

NINE DO-IT-YOURSELF ENERGY EXPERIMENTS THAT PROVE YOUR THOUGHTS CREATE YOUR REALITY

PAM GROUT

INSIGHTS

HAY HOUSE, INC.

Carlsbad, California • New York City
London • Sydney • Johannesburg
Vancouver • New Delhi

Library of Congress Control Number: 2012942902

Tradepaper ISBN: 978-1-4019-3890-1
Digital ISBN: 978-1-4019-3891-8

18 17
1st edition, January 2013

Printed in the United States of America

SUSTAINABLE FORESTRY INITIATIVE

Certified Chain of Custody
Promoting Sustainable Forestry
www.sfiprogram.org
SFI-01268

SFI label applies to the text stock

For Roosky.
May your light forever shine.

CONTENTS

FOREWORD

When I was a kid, I asked my Sunday-school teacher why miracles occurred in biblical times, but didn't seem to be part of our lives today. She had no answer, and I gradually came to assume that God, church, and religious stuff were irrelevant and far removed from my own life (even though I never quit longing for something more). I left spirituality behind to pursue science, which at least made an attempt to explain how the world works.

It is a real treat to find Pam Grout's writings, which help doubters like me fill that desire for spirituality. She presents (in a delightful, fun way, at a level anyone can understand) that energy, power, and yes, even miracles are here, now, and available to everyone. The ideas and experiments in this book have helped me grasp, in language that makes sense, many of the things spiritual guides have been teaching for thousands of years.

I highly recommend this book to anyone who is seeking to understand spiritual ideas and how they apply to all of us, even someone like me with doubts about organized religion. As she points out, retraining the mind is much like potty-training a puppy—you have to keep taking it back outside and pointing out the beauty, the majesty, and the truth. Through simple, delightful baby steps, she guides the reader into awareness that miracles still happen, and that there is an amazing energy source available to everyone.

— Joyce Barrett, Ph.D.
Former NASA biologist

"The way we have been perceiving life needs to be rolled away, so that which is true can appear."

— MICHELE LONGO O'DONNELL,
CREATOR OF *LIVING BEYOND DISEASE*

PREFACE

*"Everyone who is seriously involved in the
pursuit of science becomes convinced that a spirit
is manifest in the laws of the universe—a spirit
vastly superior to that of man."*

— ALBERT EINSTEIN,
GERMAN THEORETICAL PHYSICIST

Two months before I turned 35, my longtime boyfriend dumped me for a 20-something law student with dark roots. Keep in mind that this was about the same time the single woman/asteroid study came out, the one that publicly revealed that women over 30 have roughly the same odds of walking down the nuptial aisle as they do of being sideswiped by an asteroid.

After several days of lying in bed and staring at my ceiling fan, I came to the conclusion that I had two choices left. I could either slit my veins in a warm bath . . . or sign up for a month-long work-study program at Esalen, the self-improvement mecca in Big Sur, California. Knowing how my roommate at the time despised messes, I opted for Esalen.

On the second night there, I met a handsome former surfer named Stan who convinced me to spend the evening listening to the ocean crashing against the cliffs. We finally fell asleep in one of the massage rooms, huddled together to stay warm. Not that it worked. April winds off the Pacific can be ferocious, and even with our combined body heat we practically froze to death. Come to think of it, it would certainly have solved my messy suicide dilemma.

If Stan hadn't been so cute and I hadn't been so desperate to get over the jerk who'd tossed me aside like some empty bag of Doritos, I probably would have excused myself and gone back to my insulated sleeping bag. But I stayed until the next morning when the "dawn's early light" revealed that the whole time there'd been a space heater next to the mat where we'd been huddled. A space heater we could have turned on and used to keep warm!

In a nutshell, that's what this book is about. There's a space heater—or rather an invisible energy force—that's constantly available for our use, and we haven't bothered to turn it on. Most of us are totally oblivious to the fact the "space heater" even exists. We think of life as a random crapshoot. *C'est la vie.*

Those of us who *do* know about the space heater (that is, the energetic field that gives us the ability to shape and design our lives) don't understand how it works. We've heard rumors that praying turns it on, that good works keep it going. But no one seems to know for sure. This guru tells us to chant. The next one suggests meditation. The one from last year insisted we clean up our thoughts and increase our vibrations. So which is it? Is the energy force really that vague and mysterious? And why does it only work sometimes? At best, it's finicky and fickle, certainly nothing you can bank on.

Or is it?

What I'd like to suggest is that this invisible energy field is 100 percent reliable. It works every time, like a math principle or a law of physics. Two plus two *always* equals four. Balls dropped off roofs *always* fall. Your every thought *always* affects physical reality.

Seeing Is Believing

"My fingers are being pried off all I think I know.
Certainty is very useful, but it can really close
your mind off to the true light."

— DAVID O. RUSSELL, AMERICAN FILMMAKER

If you've read *The Secret* or been in metaphysical, spiritual circles for any time at all, you already know your thoughts create your reality, that there's a power in the universe that can heal, and that you and you alone design your own life. Unfortunately, there's still this tiny little problem, this one itty-bitty catch.

You don't *really* believe it. Not fully.

Most of us, in fact, are still operating out of the mental architecture of our ancestors. We think we're running our lives with our brilliant ideas and thoughts. We think we're affirming our intentions and creating new possibilities, but in reality we're simply recycling old tapes, knee-jerk conditioning, and automatic behaviors, most of which we picked up before we were five. We're like Pavlov's dogs, simply reacting to patterns we picked up before we had the intelligence to wisely choose. Most of the thoughts we assume are our own are really the invisible and largely unquestioned beliefs we downloaded from others. So we pit our positive thoughts against our old, disempowering programming. In other words, our consciousness, that force that *always* affects physical reality, has been hijacked.

Not long after I graduated from college, landed a job, and was running my own affairs, I noticed negative thoughts about money dive-bombing for my attention. I found myself worrying, wondering if running out of money was imminent, questioning whether or not I could afford the new bike I wanted or the new computer I needed. One day, during an early-morning jog, I suddenly got it. Those thoughts were exact clones of comments my mother often made when I was growing up. And even though there was no evidence to support those fears in my own life, I had downloaded them straight into my consciousness without even being aware of it.

Needless to say, that wasn't a paradigm that served my highest good. I consciously rewrote the paradigm that ran my financial life to: "I can afford anything I want. In fact, I am so prosperous I never need worry again." As an independent freelance writer, I also appointed God as the CEO of my career. I figured there was no way I could run this fickle writing business with the faulty wiring and negative thoughts I'd downloaded from my past. Clearly, I needed a new energetic imprint.

Reality's Changed, Dude!

> *"If we worked on the assumption that what is accepted as true really is true, then there would be little hope for advance."*

— ORVILLE WRIGHT, AMERICAN INVENTOR

Even though the reductionist, mechanical worldview has been proved defective, it's still deeply ingrained and embedded into our culture. Neuroscientists tell us that 95 percent of our thoughts are controlled by our preprogrammed subconscious mind. Instead of actually thinking, you're looking at a "movie" of the past.

If you weren't immersed in this nonstop riot of fragmented, old-school thinking, you'd be modifying your life at will. You'd have no fear around money, you'd have nothing but beautiful relationships, and you'd be so ecstatically content that it would never occur to you to pick up a book like this.

Quite frankly, I'm glad you did. This little book will prove to you once and for all that your thoughts have power and that a field of infinite possibilities awaits your claim. It will help you rewrite the outdated thinking that drives your life.

Instead of making a grand argument, the same grand argument you've read about in all the other books about changing reality, this book has nine easy-to-try experiments that offer real-time proof. It gives you the opportunity to move from "knowing" your thoughts create reality to witnessing it happen on a daily, decision-by-decision basis.

At this point, it's still a theory. Seeing with your own two eyes that you change reality simply by observing it will rewire your brain and divest you from old conditioning. Learning, through scientific experimentation, how deeply you are connected to the field of potentiality will literally set you free.

The Magic We Threw Overboard

"Oh my, how the world still dearly loves a cage."

— TESS LYNCH,

WRITER, GENTLEWOMAN, AND ESSAYIST

xix

Quantum physics defines the field as "invisible moving forces that influence the physical realm." In this book, you'll learn to use this field of potentiality (I like to call it the *FP*) to your advantage. Because energy is invisible and because we're still operating from old-school principles that put materiality first, we haven't learned to truly harness this fundamental building block.

For the next 21 days, roughly the time it takes to do the experiments in this book, you have the rare opportunity to develop a conscious relationship with energy (even matter, said quantum physicist David Bohm, is nothing but "frozen light") and learn to transform and parlay it into anything your heart desires—whether it be peace of mind, money, or a more rewarding career. You can even direct the FP to provide a vacation to Tahiti.

Take me, for example. A few years ago, I decided to spend a month in Australia. A chiropractor I had a huge crush on had just taken a job there to work with Aborigines. How, I wondered, were we going to fall in love when I was in Kansas and he was 10,683 miles away? One look at my bank statement would have convinced any reasonable person that a $1,500 plane ticket to Sydney, the going price at that time, was out of the question. But I wanted to go, and I was lucky enough to know about the field of potentiality that could make that happen.

I started planning the trip, began picturing myself romping through the Sydney surf. I mean I got really worked up over this picture in my mind.

Within a week, my editor at *Modern Bride* magazine called.

"I know it's late notice," she began, "but is there any way you'd be willing to go to Australia to write a honeymoon story? We'll pay extra."

"Well, okay," I said. "If you insist."

You can transform energy to heal and change your body. I was hiking with a friend in the flatlands near Steamboat Springs, Colorado. Climbing up the one path in the entire park, she tripped over a rock, fell, and watched in horror as her ankle started swelling. I mean, this ankle *swelled.* It wouldn't have been a problem if this had happened next door to a free health clinic, but keep in mind the two of us were 70 minutes (and that's if you walk fast, which she couldn't do because she was limping) from the nearest phone connection, let alone a free health clinic. I told her to direct her body to quit swelling. She started yelling, "Stop swelling! Heal! Stop Swelling! Heal!"

"It's okay to say it quietly," I reminded her.

We made it to our camp, and she never even had to see a doctor.

FP = IP (Infinite Potentiality)

"Life is waiting everywhere, the future is flowering everywhere, but we only see a small part of it and step on much of it with our feet."

— HERMANN HESSE,
GERMAN-SWISS POET AND NOVELIST

The nine experiments in this book, most of which take a short 48 hours or less, will prove that the FP, like electricity, is dependable, predictable, and available to everyone from St. Francis of Assisi to Barbara Walters. They'll prove what physicists over the past 100 years have discovered— that the field connects all of us, and that the reason we control our lives is because every thought we have is an energy wave that affects everything else in the universe.

But, like electricity, you *do* have to plug into it. And you do have to quit being so gosh-darned wishy-washy. Nobody in his or her right mind would call up Sears and say, "Oh, just send me something I like." Likewise, you wouldn't call a plumber to fix your toilet with this proviso: "Just come whenever you feel like it." Yet that's how most of us interact with the field. We're wimpy, vague, and don't have a clue how it actually works.

E-Squared not only explains how the FP works, but it provides nine experiments, each of which can be conducted with absolutely no money and very little time expenditure, to prove that thoughts are actual physical "things." Yes, you read that right. It says *prove.*

The nine energy principles presented in this book will confirm that the FP is at work in your life whether you're aware of its existence or not. You'll learn that it's more profound than physical laws and every bit as dependable as gravity—once you learn to be definite and crystal clear in your intentions. And agree to set deadlines. And get over this crazy illusion that something—you're never even sure what—is wrong with you. To effectively work these spiritual laws, you have to "get it" deep down in your bones that the universe is bountiful and that, at all times, it has your back.

I don't remember the exact moment I started conducting do-it-yourself experiments with my life. I do know it had become increasingly clear to me that all the spiritual theories and books and classes that I was so fascinated with were basically worthless without my full participation.

Like most people, I started with baby steps—making simple intentions like securing up-front parking spots, finding four-leaf clovers, getting interviews with people in the headlines. But the "result" that finally convinced me that setting up a framework, posing a deadline, and using scientific-style experimentation was imperative to real spiritual growth was what I now refer to as the nail miracle.

For years, I hung a calendar beside my bed, plucking it down from time to time to jot down important events or to look back for the date I last cut my hair or met so-and-so or went to the dentist. One night, I grabbed the calendar a bit too eagerly and pulled out the small nail that secured it to the wall. I got down on my hands and knees to search for it. How far can a little nail go, right? I looked and I looked and I looked. Apparently, that little nail had secured a Harry Potter–style invisibility cloak, because it was nowhere to be found.

I finally concluded that I had spent enough time crawling around on my carpet and that I would just send out an intention for it to show up. Within 24 hours.

The next morning when I woke up, the nail was in my hand nestled between my thumb and forefinger. Since then, I've gone on to manifest all sorts of cool things— from dates with hot guys to a regular travel-writing gig to a Toyota Prius—but none of them made the kind of impression that the simple little nail did.

I was getting such convincing results with my own experiments that I decided it was time to reproduce them, to see if they'd work as well for others. I began suggesting some of these simple experiments to friends. One colleague, a Unity minister, had her whole congregation using the lab reports you'll find at the end of each chapter.

Before long, YOU'ers (that's Youth of Unity) were visibly moving energy around with their homemade Einstein wands. Weekly groups were being formed to conduct regular experiments. People were manifesting all sorts of amazing things.

What I know for sure is that the best way to understand a spiritual principle, maybe the only way, is not to read about it in a book or to hear a speaker explain it from a podium, but to put it into a framework that demonstrates how it works. Seeing it in action, as you will in these experiments, leads to complete and certain conviction. And that's the only thing that will radically release you from "old-school" mental architecture.

The New Curriculum

"I have to find it here, right here, bursting uncontainably through the slipshod, dragged down dead center of one ordinary life. . . ."

— BOB SAVINO, POET AND KANSAS CITY SAGE

1. The Dude Abides Principle. This is the basic principle, the foundation upon which all the others rest. Basically what it says is, "There is an invisible energy force or field of infinite possibilities." The experiment could best be described as an ultimatum. You're going to give the force exactly 48 hours to make its presence known. You're going to demand a clear, unmistakable sign, something that cannot be written off as coincidence.

2. The Volkswagen Jetta Principle. Remember that new car you bought a few years ago? When you first decided it was the car of your dreams, it seemed like a unique car. You figured you'd be the only one in town to proudly drive one. Well, by the time you read up on it in *Consumer Reports,* decided on the price you needed to offer, and finally got yourself to the car dealership, you noticed that practically every eighth car was a Volkswagen Jetta or whatever car it was you wanted. And that's what happens when you begin to think about something—you draw it into your life.

Every thought we have, every judgment we make, impacts the field of potentiality. In fact, reality is nothing but waves of possibility that we have "observed" into form. This principle states, "You impact the field and draw from it according to your beliefs and expectations," and to prove it we'll set the following clear intention: "This is what I want to pull out of the field in the next 48 hours."

3. The Alby Einstein Principle. Even though this principle, "You, too, are a field of energy," is one of the cornerstone spiritual principles, it actually first came to light in a physics lab. Yes, it was scientists who discovered that, despite all appearances to the contrary, human beings are not matter, but continually moving waves of energy. In fact, you probably noticed the title of this book is a play on Einstein's famous equation.

This is the only experiment that involves equipment—specially designed, perfectly tuned equipment. Okay, so it's a metal coat hanger (a specimen of which I'm assuming, unless you're a complete and total slob, is available in your closet) and a drinking straw, something you can easily score free of charge at any McDonald's.

4. The Abracadabra Principle. Most people associate the word *abracadabra* with magicians pulling rabbits out of hats. It's actually an Aramaic term that translates into English as, "I will create as I speak." It's a powerful concept. It's why Edison often announced the invention of a device before he'd actually invented it. It's why Jim Carrey wrote himself a check for $10 million long before he ever made a movie.

This principle simply says, "Whatever you focus on expands," and in the experiment you'll learn that there's no such thing as an idle thought and that all of us are way too cavalier and tolerant of our minds' wandering.

5. The Dear Abby Principle. This principle states: "Your connection to the field provides accurate and unlimited guidance." By realigning your consciousness, you can access reliable answers to every request you ever make. The reason you don't know this is because you've taught yourself the most unnatural habit of feeling separate, of not being in communion with the FP.

6. The Superhero Principle. In this experiment, governed by the principle "Your thoughts and consciousness impact matter," you will duplicate an experiment conducted by Dr. Gary Schwartz, a professor at the University of Arizona, which demonstrated that sending intention to plants made them grow faster and reflect more light than their nonintentioned counterparts.

7. The Jenny Craig Principle. Whether you're a label reader or not, you know the food you eat offers certain vitamins, minerals, and of course, calories. You probably think these nutrients are cut-and-dried, that if the back of the yogurt container says it has 187 calories, then it has 187 calories. What you may not know is that your thoughts about yourself and your food are in a constant dance with your body. And that when you feel guilty about consuming calories, your food picks up a negative vibe that ricochets right back at you. In this experiment, you'll prove the principle "Your thoughts and consciousness provide the scaffolding for your physical body" by infusing your food with love.

8. The 101 Dalmatians Principle. This all-important spiritual principle states: "You are connected to everything and everyone else in the universe." Scientists call it nonlocality, and if you watched the cartoon version of *101 Dalmatians,* you saw the principle in action. Remember when Cruella De Vil's evil cohorts were trying to capture the escaped puppies? The old Scottish terrier in the barn where they were hiding barked for help to a basset hound in the next county, who, in turn, barked the message to a dachshund farther along the route. Only in quantum physics, the communication happens instantaneously. The very instant the Scottish terrier knows that the puppies require help, the dachshund, 20 miles away, also knows. Anything that happens to one particle is instantaneously communicated to the other. In this experiment, you'll send messages to people in other places without the use of e-mail, letters, or loud explosions.

9. The Fish and Loaves Principle. This principle states: "The universe is limitless, abundant, and strangely accommodating." It will also prove that your fears are pointless and that maybe it's okay to take a big, deep breath.

A Truer, Grander Vision

"You can never change things by fighting the existing reality. To change something, build a new model that makes the existing model obsolete."

— BUCKMINSTER FULLER, AMERICAN FUTURIST

I hope it's comforting to know that you won't be the first to use your life as an experiment. When the late, great R. Buckminster Fuller was 32, he decided to conduct an experiment to see what one penniless unknown individual might be able to do on behalf of humanity. Dubbing himself Guinea Pig B, he dedicated himself to bringing about change in the world.

At the time he started the experiment, he was what you might call a "nobody." Bankrupt and unemployed, he had a wife and baby to support. His first child, the baby's older sister, had just died. He had been drinking heavily.

His prospects didn't look promising. But he decided to cast aside the past, to give up limiting thoughts. He wanted to know, "What could one person do to change the world?"

For the next 56 years, he devoted himself to his unique experiment. He took risks. He asked, "What if?"

Not only did he become an architect, an inventor, an author, and a great leader of men, but between 1927, when he launched the experiment, and his death in 1983, he wrote 28 books, received 44 honorary degrees, registered 25 U.S. patents, and literally changed the way humans see themselves.

That's what I hope *E-Squared* will do for you. I hope it will change the way you see yourself. I hope it will inspire you to conduct an experiment with your own life, to use your energy to become the most fantastic, the most joyful, wondrous, beautiful, tender human being you possibly can.

INTRODUCTION

Collapse of the Wave:
Where We Learn We Are Badly Misinformed

"Man's chief delusion is his conviction that there are causes other than his own state of consciousness."
— NEVILLE GODDARD, BARBADIAN AUTHOR AND MYSTIC

Any illusionist worth his magic wand understands that the most important ingredient in his sleight-of-hand repertoire is diversion. A magician diverts his audience's attention *away* from what he's really doing and directs it *toward* something else that seems crucial but, of course, isn't.

That's what we've done—diverted all our attention to the physical world. These sensory "bluffs" have caused us to miss the fact that what is invisible, what we *can't* see with our eyes, is actually more fundamental to life than what we do see.

Quantum physics tells us that the invisible energy realm—collectively referred to as the field, or the "FP," as I call it—is the primary governing force of the material realm. It's the blueprint that forms reality. Indeed, we now know that the universe is made of nothing but waves and particles of energy that conform to our expectations, judgments, and beliefs.

Subtle energies, thoughts, emotions, and consciousness play the starring roles in our life experiences, but because they're invisible, we haven't attempted to understand them or use them in our favor. To change the world is a simple matter of changing these expectations and beliefs. It's truly that easy. To bring something into the physical world requires focusing not on what we see, but on what we *want* to see.

Good, Good, Good, Good Vibrations

> *"'El Niño of human consciousness' has arrived."*
>
> — Dianne Collins, author of *Do You Quantum Think?*

Okay, just say it: "How can something as simple as a thought influence the world?" Let me just point out that a hundred years ago nobody would have believed songs sung by a bunch of *American Idol* contestants could pass through brick, glass, wood, and steel to get from a transmitter tower to your television set, either. Nobody would have believed a cell phone no bigger than a deck of cards would allow you to talk to your sister 2,000 miles away.

Your thoughts, like the 289 TV channels and like your voice on the cell phone, are vibrational waves. When you hear Eminem rapping about his daughter Hailie, your eardrum is catching a vibrational sound wave. When you see Brad Pitt's cane or Madonna's single leather glove (accessories they sported at the 2012 Golden Globes), you're seeing patterns of vibrational light waves.

And that's what your thoughts are—vibrational energy waves that interact and influence the FP. Every thought you have, have ever had, or ever will have creates a vibration that goes out into the FP, extending forever. These vibrations meet other vibrations, crisscrossing in an incredible maze of energy. Get enough energy together and it clumps into matter. Remember what Einstein said—matter is formed out of energy.

The field of potentiality simply follows the energy you send out. And your thought vibrations draw other vibrations that match. Here's one small example: A few years ago, I wanted a potato masher. I didn't mention it to anyone. I just made a mental note: *Next time you're at Walmart, buy a potato masher.* That very night, my friend Wendy, who was cleaning out her drawers, stopped by with a couple of no-longer-needed cooking utensils, including a potato masher. Another time, I decided I needed more laughter in my life. Within a couple weeks, I began dating Todd, a funny co-worker who eventually became a comedian.

The coincidences we see in our lives are just energy and the FP at work. Most of the time, we employ energy inadvertently, totally oblivious to the fact that what we think, say, and do makes a difference. Consequently, we activate this limitless power to follow a default program that makes no use of imagination or possibility.

People think Jesus is the be-all and end-all, because he was so good at manipulating energy and matter. But, as he so poignantly pointed out (although these aren't his exact words), "You, too, are da' man."

I'm a single mom, not exactly the best "stereotype" in which to be cast. Like being black or Jewish, it brings up certain preconceived notions. People automatically expect me to be poor, maybe on welfare.

While that's certainly one of the available channels, I prefer to watch a different channel. I prefer to focus on a different reality.

Here's what it says on my website: "Pam Grout is a world traveler, a loving mother, a best-selling author, a millionaire, and an inspiring witness to everyone she meets." I started focusing on those things 20 years ago, before I'd ever had a child, before I became a world traveler or an author, and for that matter, before I even liked myself all that much. Focusing on what I wanted obviously worked, because now I can proudly say that all but one of the above are true. I'll let you guess which one is yet to manifest. So far, I've written 16 books, two screenplays, a live soap opera, and enough magazine articles that I haven't starved in 20 years without a 9-to-5 job. I maintain a travel blog (**www.georgeclooneyslepthere.com**) that has taken me to all seven continents. I've written about everything from bungee jumping in New Zealand to carpet buying in Morocco to picking coffee in Nicaragua.

I have yet to jump out of an airplane, but I have to save something for my 90th birthday.

The First Step in Spiritual Enlightenment: Give Up Your Powerful Attachment to Conventional Reality

"We are all captives of a story."

— DANIEL QUINN, AUTHOR OF *ISHMAEL*

Reality ain't all it's cracked up to be.

In fact, it's not a stretch to say that everything you think is real is not. Physicists, for going on 100 years now, have not known what to make of the fact that Newton's classical view of the world has absolutely no bearing on the way the world works at its core. The subatomic realm so defies all reason and logic that most scientists, scared to endanger their academic credentials, have more or less ignored the fact that life is nothing like what we pretend it is.

In fact, it's so freaky—particles popping up out of nowhere, time slowing down and speeding up, particles reacting and communicating with each other even when separated by thousands of miles—that the only thing scientists have done with this information so far is develop technology that allows us to blow each other up, send text messages, receive cell-phone messages, and nuke our Hungry-Man TV dinners.

Even the two main fundaments of physical reality— space and time—are not what they seem. These two physical mainstays are nothing but extremely convincing optical illusions. Physicists like Bernard d'Espagnat, recent winner of the $1.4 million Templeton Prize, tell us it's high time we trade in our old formulation of natural law for a radically different, more accurate view of reality: namely, that consciousness itself creates the material world.

Even though every physicist on the planet knows about the freaky universe where matter pops into existence from nothing at all and where electrons can jump from one orbit to another without traveling across intervening space, most have chosen to ignore it, to shrug their shoulders, and to employ the old tween standby "Whatever!"

It's not that they're in total denial. As I mentioned, they've used the new physics to develop lasers, transistors, superconductors, and atom bombs. But they can't even begin to explain how this quantum world works. As physicist James Trefil observed, "We've encountered an area of the universe our brains just aren't wired to understand."

A few brave physicists are starting to acknowledge that their precious assumptions may be wrong. They're admitting that the fundamental tenets of material reality just don't hold up. Some are even brave enough to admit that consciousness itself creates the physical world. (As Dr. Fred Alan Wolf, a physicist popularly known as Dr. Quantum, says, "It boils down to this—the universe doesn't exist without a perceiver of that universe.")

All I have to say is, "About time."

A Course in Miracles, a self-study program in spiritual psychology that I've been practicing and teaching for 25 years, has always advocated the idea that consciousness creates the material world. It says we humans decide in advance how we're going to experience life, that we choose beforehand what we want to see.

The problem is, we all look at the world with a giant chip on our shoulder. All we need to do to change the course of our crummy lives is to get over our ongoing grudge against the world, to actively see and expect a different reality. As it is now, we devote all our time and attention (our consciousness, if you will) to things we do not want.

But it's nothing more than a bad habit. And like any bad habit, it can be changed with conscious and deliberate effort.

It Is What It Isn't

"Man's concept of his world built on the experience of the five senses is no longer adequate and in many cases no longer valid."

— Shafica Karagulla, M.D.,
Turkish-born psychiatrist

Right now, the planet you call home is spinning at a rate of roughly 930 miles per hour. It's orbiting the sun at an astonishing 66,486 miles per hour. But unless you just polished off a couple pitchers of beer, you probably aren't aware of any such movement. That's just one tiny example of how we distort reality.

Turns out that almost all the concepts and judgments we take for granted are distortions. Very early on—say, sometime around birth—our minds establish a pattern of perception and then proceed to filter out everything else. In other words, we only "experience" things that jibe with our very limited perception.

A girl from the Philippines told me it was weeks, if not months, after she arrived in the United States before she noticed that some people here had red hair, including people she knew and dealt with on a regular basis. Red hair was inconsistent with what she had been conditioned to see and expect. So for several months, she was subjectively blind to red hair, seeing it as the brunette of her culture.

Scientists now know the brain receives 400 billion bits of information each second. To give you some idea of just how much information that is, consider this: It would take nearly 600,000 average-size books just to print 400 billion zeros. Needless to say, that's a heck of a lot of reality. So what do we do? We start screening. We start narrowing down. *I'll take that bit of information over there, and let's see—this one fits nicely with my ongoing soap opera about the opposite sex.* When all is said and done, we're down to 2,000 measly bits of information. Go ahead and take a bow, because even that's pretty impressive. We're talking 2,000 bits of information each and every second. But here's the problem. What we choose to take in is only one-half of one-millionth of a percent of what's out there.

Let's pretend that each dot of a pen point is one bit of information. I've been practicing, and the most dots I can reasonably make in one second is five. But let's be generous and assume you're a better pen dotter than I am—let's pretend you can make ten dots per second. Again, we're assuming each dot is a bit of information. To make as many dots as your brain processes in one second takes nearly three and a half minutes at your highly superior rate of ten dots per second. But if your brain were processing all the available information (400 billion dots), it would take 821 years!

Our brains continually sift through the possibilities and pick which bits of information to "see" and believe. Out of sheer laziness, the stuff we choose to perceive—and make no mistake . . . it *is* a choice—is stuff we already know. It's stuff we decided on way back when. We see, feel, taste, touch, and smell not the real world, but a drastically condensed version of the world, a version that our brains literally concoct. The rest zooms by without recognition. John Maunsell, a neuroscientist at Harvard University, says, "People imagine they're seeing what's really there, but they're not."

Once your brain decides which bits to let in, it builds bridges between various nerve cells, interlacing nerve fibers to create neural pathways. The average human has 100 billion nerve cells, each with innumerable extensions, so different highways get built in each brain. The map of neural pathways in your brain and, say, Johnny Depp's brain are as different as the maps of Wisconsin and Rhode Island.

Once you get the pathways set up, you quit traveling the rest of the country. Interstate 70 in my home state of Kansas makes for a perfect metaphor. Believe it or not, Kansas—the state *The Wizard of Oz* portrayed in black and white—actually contains lots of geological landmarks. There's a miniature Grand Canyon in the northwest corner, for example, and a huge seven-story limestone formation called Castle Rock near the town of Quinter. But since people traveling through Kansas rarely leave I-70, nobody has a clue that these geological formations exist. They've literally bypassed all the beautiful, worthwhile stuff and come to the erroneous conclusion that Kansas is flat and boring. But it's not reality.

Like those highway planners who put I-70 on the flattest, quickest, and easiest route, we build our neural pathways on the least complicated routes—the ones we've traveled so many times before. But this doesn't show us reality. Not even close. We don't begin to see all that is there—only three and a half minutes, compared to 821 years.

The roads and highways of our brains get set up pretty early. When we're born, every possibility exists. Let's take language, for example. Within every newborn is the ability to pronounce every sound in every single language. The potential is there for the *r* rolling of the Spanish language. It's also there for those guttural German diphthongs.

But very early on, our brains lay down neural pathways that mesh with the sounds we hear every day, eliminating other sounds from other languages.

With the possible exception of Barbara Walters, pretty much everyone who speaks English can pronounce the following phrase: "Rolling Rock really rouses Roland Ratinsky." But when people from China try to learn English, they no longer have the neural pathways to properly say their *r*'s, so that's why "fried rice" becomes "flied lice." Just so no one thinks I'm ethnocentric, I should probably add that I've tried pronouncing some of those guttural German words only to discover that my German neural pathways have been shot to hell and back.

Perhaps the best example of how your mind creates its own virtual-reality game is the everyday, garden-variety dream. When Morley Safer showed up on your doorstep last night asking all those embarrassing questions, it seemed pretty darn real. But once the alarm clock went off, Morley and that virtual *60 Minutes* interview popped like the flimsy soap bubble it was.

Our neural pathways establish reruns of what has gone on before. Like the three-year-old who insists on watching *The Little Mermaid* over and over and over again, we cling to our warped illusions with a tenacious grip. *Get your bloody hands off my illusion!* Even though it makes us miserable, we prefer to place our faith in the disaster we have made.

We Observe Things into Form

> "It takes zero faith. What it takes is imagination.
> . . . If it's clear in your thought, it is even this moment
> barreling down on you like a Mack truck."
>
> — RICHARD BACH, AUTHOR OF *ILLUSIONS*
> AND OTHER METAPHYSICAL NOVELS

If you ask me, learning how to transform energy is so important it should be taught along with reading, writing, and arithmetic. And it all starts with intent, the force that lies behind everything. It's the energy, the fuel, the electric charge that sets up a resonant field and sends out probability waves into the FP. Esther Hicks, who facilitates the Abraham-Hicks material, calls it "launching a rocket of desire." Giving it attention adds mass.

The minute you make an intention, you create it. It's instantaneous. It exists as an actual thing. You don't see it yet because you're still operating from linear time. You're still sold on the old-school adage "creating things takes time." So you keep working and waiting. You keep following the seven steps from the latest self-help book.

But here's what physicists tell us. Things, in the quantum world, do not happen in steps. They happen immediately.

So the thing you intend, the minute you intend it, exists, but like Schrödinger's cat, a famous thought experiment devised in 1935 by Austrian physicist Erwin Schrödinger, you're only aware of the reality you choose to observe. The physical manifestation remains enfolded outside your current consciousness.

Cutting-edge physicists tells us life is multidimensional. But most of us are stuck in our one-dimensional physical reality, restricted to what we experience with our five senses. What we experience with these alleged foolproof tools of observation are nothing but what we decide to look for. It's not even a chicken-or-egg question. What we see, experience, and feel with our five senses always comes after the decision to see, experience, and feel it.

I liken consciousness to a giant skyscraper. I may be living on the second floor, but the "thing" I created with my thought is up on the 17th floor. Until I can get to the 17th floor, it appears it's still missing, that I'm still waiting.

Another great analogy is a television set. If you have cable, more than 100 channels are yours for the clicking. TiVo aside, you can only watch one channel at a time. When you're watching, say, *Modern Family,* you're chuckling at the antics of Cam, Mitchell, Phil, and Gloria and you're completely unaware of the other 99 (or more) channels. That's why it's really important to stay on the channel you want. Don't give any airtime to the reality from which you're trying to escape. Tune in only to your intent.

Reasons We Dial into Programs We Don't Like

"We live in a world that worships limitations."

— Tama Kieves, author of *This Time I Dance!*

1. We're not really here—not in "this moment." The now is the point of power. That's why it's so easy for a yogi, who consciously clears out mental static, to change his heart rate, pulse, and other body functions. If you're not really here, your mind is not available to do what you're asking it to do. It's imperative to practice conscious, moment-by-moment awareness. Otherwise, you're operating out of old encrusted beliefs, beliefs you downloaded before you were five years old. Do you really want a five-year-old running your life?

When I find my consciousness operating outside "the now," which is unfortunately a great percentage of the time, I gently remind myself of this analogy: The UPS driver just delivered to my house every single thing I've ever wanted, but because I've left the building, I don't even realize it. I'm out hunting for paltry substitutes. Everything is right there, once I bring my consciousness back to the timelessness of "now."

2. We've named it difficult. The power to create with our thoughts is a piece of cake. That's not even up for debate. But we keep telling our friends and especially ourselves that it's hard or that we're still working on it. Just notice in the next couple of days how often you affirm that it's "hard" or "challenging." Pay attention to how often you say, "Things have always been like that," or "It runs in my family." We spend so much time talking about what doesn't work that we miss the whole point: namely, that we have the power to create something that *does.*

3. We stalk negativity. What do we study? Disease, problems, disasters of the past. What do we prepare for? Emergencies. We love to sink our teeth into problems and ask, "What's wrong?" It's an old-school model that sorely needs transformation. Once we begin to look for what's right, our lives begin spinning in unimaginably exciting new directions.

And here's the truth. Every "wrong" thing, which in reality is nothing but a foolhardy judgment, has a flip side. Lack is the flip side of abundance. Sickness is the flip side of health. Both ideas exist at the same time. Both are true. By choosing to see one aspect, the other equally likely aspect is hidden.

Unfortunately, while living in the consciousness of space and time, you can only observe one side of the coin at a time. But it's important to realize that the other side is just as real and that at any time, you can simply flip it over.

Opposites (for example, abundance/lack) are both true. It's a question of which reality you'd rather live from.

4. By George, we think we've got it. Once you define something, you no longer question it. Once you know something, it becomes your reality. But knowing anything is exceedingly restrictive. In quantum speak, it collapses the wave, leaving no room for mystery, wonder, and new discoveries. Think about it. If one of your arms is filled with books and the other with a bag of groceries, it's impossible to pick up anything else. You may have a lot of knowledge and a bunch of academic degrees, framed and hanging on the second floor of that skyscraper. But remember there are lots of other "floors" (that is, dimensions) and all that you "know" can block potentialities.

5. The mind is *so* powerful it can create something "outside" itself to be *more* powerful. That's why it's essential when doing the experiments to suspend judgment long enough to believe they'll work. If you're convinced they're a family-size bucket of bull, you'll collect data to support that viewpoint.

6. We haven't really practiced. Using the FP to direct your life is not an intellectual exercise. It's not a theory. It's a practice. Like mastering scales. Or learning to play Ping-Pong. Tiger Woods may have only been 18 when he won the U.S. Amateur Championship, but he'd already racked up 16 years of practice. And he still devotes many hours a day to conditioning and practice. You cannot know wisdom. You can only be wisdom. And that's where this book comes in.

Picking Another Channel

*"Emancipate yourself from mental slavery.
None but ourselves can free our minds."*

— MARCUS GARVEY, JAMAICAN POLITICAL LEADER
AND MENTOR TO BOB MARLEY

The purpose of this book is to release you from the imprisonment of your illusions, to help you set aside the manufactured press release you believe to be reality. The good news is you don't have to change a single one of your behaviors. All you have to do is change your mind.

In case you haven't checked Amazon lately, there are literally thousands of books on how to change your body. At last count, "buns" alone merited 678 books and CDs. But as far as I can tell, there's not a single book on how to shape your mind. Yet your mind, with all its preset, misconstrued neural pathways, is the root of all your problems. Remember that it is consciousness, as brave physicists such as Fred Wolf are starting to acknowledge, that creates physical reality. Even those buns that aren't steel yet.

You can go back time and time again to the shoe store, but it will never sell milk. And all those desperate attempts to change your body, your relationship, your fill-in-the-blank are never going to work until you learn to change and shape your mind.

It's pretty difficult to control your mind when you think you have to do it forever. But by setting up a defined time frame, as you will in the experiments in this book, your mind can be coaxed into giving it a whirl. It's like a 12-step program. Trying to stay sober forever can't work. One day at a time? Now, that's something a mind can wrap itself around.

All but two of the experiments take 48 hours or less. That's two short days out of a 70-plus-year life span. Even a flabby mind can commit to that. Why do I give you 48 hours? Call it the old deadline principle. When an editor gives a deadline, he or she knows to start checking for said manuscript around that time. Deadlines give us something to expect, something to look for. When you're on an unfamiliar country road looking for the green mailbox where you're supposed to turn left to your blind date's house, it helps to know it's 8.1 miles from the last turn. Otherwise, you start to wonder if you missed it and end up doubling back. A deadline simply jars you into paying attention.

Once, I asked for guidance on whether or not to begin freelance writing full-time. I was working 20 hours a week for a small company and writing on the side.

"I really like Resource and Development," I said, referring to the place I was working, "but I have this dream, you see, of being a full-time freelancer. It's not that I don't like writing fund-raising letters; it's just that I want to pursue my own story ideas, write about the things that burn in my heart. What do you think?"

Already, I was getting lots of assignments. Big national magazines were calling. I was making new contacts, receiving nibbles on a couple of column ideas. That would have been answer enough for some people.

But I'm dense. I wanted an unquestionable sign.

"Okay," I went on, "I need a sign that cannot be written off as coincidence. Furthermore, I'm imposing a specific deadline. I need to know in the next 24 hours."

The next day, I got fired.

Another time, when my freelancing was slow, I sent out résumés, something I'm prone to do whenever I feel panicky. Sure enough, I was offered a job within a few weeks.

The offer—writing marketing materials for a local bus line (okay, I didn't say I was offered an interesting job in two weeks)—was for more money than I'd ever made in my life. But how could I afford to give up all that time? Was I really ready to forgo my freelancing career? Once again, I demanded a clear sign. I needed to know within 24 hours because that's when I needed to give my employer-to-be a *yea* or a *nay*.

The very next morning, *Travel + Leisure*, the magazine I most wanted to write for, called to give me an assignment.

I hung up, shouted "Yes!" and did the goal-line hootchie-koo. But my guidance must have been in the mood to show off that day, because not 15 minutes later, another magazine I'd never even heard of, let alone sent a query to, called and wanted a story about Kansas City steaks. I had to call and tell my would-be boss, "Thanks, but no thanks."

To be in the kingdom, as *A Course in Miracles* puts it, is to merely focus your full attention on it. You have to be willing to perceive nothing else.

Currently, our minds are devoted to things we do not want. Our positive intentions occupy but a tiny sliver of our minds. The rest is focused on the problems we hope the intentions will eliminate. The majority of our brainpower is devoted to the old beliefs of scarcity, problem relationships, and a God who shoots fire bolts from heaven.

The reason 99.9 percent of your mind is still devoted to things you don't want is because that's the world's default setting, what it defines as normal. The world's default setting sees news about floods and earthquakes, hears stories about your second cousin's epilepsy, and says, "See, what did I tell you?" It's next to impossible to override the world's default setting even though you know—at least theoretically—that another way is possible.

Let's take being broke, for example. Most of us can agree we don't want to be broke. So what do we do? We devote our minds to avoiding it. We work long hours. We call our stockbrokers. We read books and articles about getting rich, fully ignoring the fact that by trying to "get" rich, we are devoting our minds to the idea that we're not already rich. Consequently, we've decided in advance to be broke.

If we simply devote our minds to feeling rich, to being grateful for all the already-apparent riches in our lives—say, our families and our wonderful friends—being broke would disappear. We only experience it because we devote our thoughts to it. That's how powerful our minds are.

My friend Carla is resolute in her belief that when you feel broke, you simply must go out shopping. Immediately. "Ya gotta kick that belief in the nuts," is how I believe she words it. I tried this once on a press trip to Mackinac Island, Michigan. I was just launching my freelance career, still not sure how this "money thing" was going to pan out. I was staying at the luxurious Grand Hotel, keenly aware that the clothes I'd shoved into my suitcase at the last minute did not live up to Jane Seymour's wardrobe in *Somewhere in Time* or even to the Grand's present-day guests daintily munching their tea biscuits on the 660-foot porch. Clearly, I was underdressed. And the five-course, men-in-coats-and-ties dinner hadn't even started.

I moseyed into the pricey gift shop, and my eyes were immediately drawn to a gorgeous teal silk dress. One surreptitious peek at the price tag was proof positive that that frock was way beyond my normal budget—four times, in fact, what I'd typically spend on a dress. That's when I knew

I had to have it. I had to "act the part" of the successful freelance writer I wanted to be. I bought that dress, knowing I was paving the way for financial success in my newly minted career.

Like Housebreaking a Puppy

> *"Everyone thinks of changing the world,*
> *but no one thinks of changing himself."*
>
> — LEO TOLSTOY, RUSSIAN NOVELIST

If your brain is anything like mine (prone to procrastination, easily confused, and distractible), changing your mind can be downright challenging. I like to think of it like housebreaking a puppy.

You just keep taking it back outside and showing it a different reality until finally it realizes, *Wow, there's a whole big world out there. And it's a lot more fun to pee on trees and bushes and fire hydrants than on Pam's ratty old house slippers.* Your mind will be astonished by the beauty that's available when you put it on the spot. Deep peace will appear. Great ideas will materialize and expand. Joy will rise up.

The only thing you need do is devote your mind *only* to things you want. If you want peace, think of peace. If you want love, think of love. If you want Jimmy Choo pumps, think of Jimmy Choo pumps. Do not think about how peace looks impossible or that love seems fleeting or that there's no money in your bank account for Jimmy Choo pumps. Keep your mind focused only on what you want. And anytime that puppy starts heading toward those slippers, pick it up and take it back outside.

In the movie *Man on Fire,* Denzel Washington plays an ex–Special Forces operative who becomes a bodyguard to the young daughter of a wealthy Mexican businessman. Despite Denzel's attempts to stay neutral and uninvolved, he ends up becoming a father figure to Pita, tutoring her with her homework and helping her gain a place on the swim team, an activity she loves more than the piano lessons her father insists upon. Over and over in their swim training, Denzel shouts out the same question: "Trained or untrained?" And Pita shouts back exuberantly, "Trained!"

So I'll repeat the question. Is your mind trained or untrained?

And I hope you'll soon be able to shout back, "Trained!"

"The greatest discovery and development of the coming years will be along spiritual lines. Here is a force which history clearly teaches has been the greatest power in the development of man and history, and yet we have been merely playing with it and have never seriously studied it as we have physical forces. Some day people will learn that material things do not bring happiness and are of little use in making men and women creative and powerful. Then the scientists of the world will turn their laboratories over to the study of the spiritual forces. When this day comes, the world will see more advancement in one generation than it has in the past four."

— CHARLES PROTEUS STEINMETZ,
INVENTOR OF THE ALTERNATING-CURRENT MOTOR

THE PRELIMINARIES

*"All life is an experiment.
The more experiments you make the better."*

— RALPH WALDO EMERSON, AMERICAN ESSAYIST

You don't need a white lab coat, carbon nanotubes, or even those unsightly protective goggles to conduct the following experiments. All you need is an open mind and the ability to observe, record your findings, and be willing to frame things in a new light.

For those of you who flunked chemistry, let's start with a refresher course.

Science Basics

"Nothing shocks me. I'm a scientist."

— ON A T-SHIRT BY DESIGNER J. BERTRAND

1. What exactly is *science?* According to Webster's, science is "knowledge attained through study or practice." It usually starts with a theory.

2. Okay, so what's a *theory?* To most of us, a theory is a vague and fuzzy fact. But when you talk about scientific theory, you're talking about a conceptual framework that explains existing observations and predicts new ones. A theory is accepted, not based on the prestige or convincing powers of its proponent, but on the results obtained through observations and/or experiments that anyone can reproduce. For example, the theory of gravity can be proved by anyone, from a toddler jumping out of a bunk bed to a voodoo priest leaping over a sacrificial goat. In fact, most lab experiments are repeated many dozens and quadrillions of times.

The other characteristic of a scientific theory is that it's falsifiable, meaning that an experiment could also prove that it's *un*true. The theory that "Mars is populated with little green men who flee whenever we hunt them" is not falsifiable because in that theory the Martians always disappear whenever anyone tracks them. But the theory that "Martians do not exist" is scientific because you can falsify it by catching one and getting him an invitation to *Good Morning America.*

3. Then what is a *hypothesis* (hy-POTH-uh-sis)? Again, in common vernacular a hypothesis is a synonym for a guess. But to a scientist, a hypothesis is a working assumption about how the world works. Every experiment starts with one. You make observations about how the world works and then you come up with a hypothesis that can be tested to see if it has truth value. It's usually cast as a

statement that can either be refuted or proved. It's often written as an "if-then" statement (if I do such and such, then such and such will happen): "If x occurs, then y will follow." Or "As x increases, so will y." We use it to form a scientific method.

4. Excuse me, a *scientific method?* The scientific method is universally accepted as being the best way for winnowing truth from lies and delusion. The simple version looks something like this:

- State a question.
- Collect information.
- Form a hypothesis.
- Test the hypothesis.
- Record and study data.
- Draw conclusions.

The great advantage of the scientific method is that it is unprejudiced. It works the same for everyone. The conclusions will hold, irrespective of your hair color, your religious persuasion, or your shoe size.

A Couple of Ground Rules

"You are doing this because you are fantastic and brave and curious. And, yes, you are probably a little crazy. And this is a good thing."

— CHRIS BATY, FOUNDER OF
NATIONAL NOVEL WRITING MONTH (NANOWRIMO)

Each of the following chapters presents an important spiritual principle and an empirical science experiment to demonstrate its validity. You can do the experiments one after another (which is what most people do, because they get so excited after the first one), or you can skip around. Do one this week. Try another next week. It's really up to you.

Before launching each experiment, make the intention to give up past conditioning. I usually start with this adage from *A Course in Miracles:* "Open your mind and clear it of all thoughts that would deceive."

And then be vigilant in receiving evidence. Look for it the same way you'd look for a set of missing car keys. On a day you're out of milk and the baby's crying. After looking everywhere you normally put them—in your purse, in the pocket of your khakis, on the counter by the door—you start lifting up couch cushions, crawling under the bed, and sifting through kitty litter. The important thing is, you don't stop looking until you're clutching them in your grubby little paws.

If you go to the grocery store for sink cleanser, you don't come home until you find the shelf with the Comet, the Ajax, and the Mr. Clean. If you go to the bookstore to pick up the latest John Grisham novel, you don't wimp out with some feeble excuse about not being able to find the "G" section. You go to the store fully knowing it's going to be there.

At the end of each chapter, there is a lab report. These are similar to the lab reports that real scientists use. It's important to jot down the time you launch each experiment. Take notes; document every finding. The more detailed the map, the better template you'll have for further study. As you log all your perceptions and experiences, be willing to risk being "wrong" in order to get the verifiable details to prove you are right.

Okay, ready to become a mad scientist?

EXPERIMENT #1

THE DUDE ABIDES PRINCIPLE:

There Is an Invisible Energy Force or Field of Infinite Possibilities

*"Everyone else is waiting for eternity
and the shamans are saying, 'How about tonight?'"*
— ALBERTO VILLOLDO, PH.D.,
CUBAN-BORN AUTHOR AND TEACHER OF ENERGY MEDICINE

The Premise

This experiment will prove to you once and for all that there is a loving, abundant, totally hip force in the universe. Some people call it God. You can call it *prana*, "the all there is," or "Cosmo Kramer," for all I care.

The problem, up until now, is we've had to take this force on faith. We weren't allowed to see it or touch it, but we've sure been asked to do lots of things in its name, like tithe and meditate and put ashes on our head. I much prefer the idea of an energy force that moves on two-way streets. Does give and take ring any bells?

In this experiment, we're going to let the FP know that, baby, it's now or never. We are *so over* believing in something that gets its jollies playing hide-and-seek. We want irrefutable proof. And we want it *now.* You know those four little initials—A.S.A.P. Well, those are the ones we're shooting for. We are going to give the FP exactly 48 hours to give us a sign, a clear sign, a sign that cannot be written off. Neon would work.

Because we bought this idea that the force is vague and mysterious, we don't really expect to find it. Or at least we're not surprised when we don't. Because we haven't been trained to notice, this inspiring, energizing, life-altering force is zooming in, around, and through us without our awareness.

What Me, Wait?

*"If your medicine doesn't grow corn,
of what use is it?"*

— Sun Bear, Chippewa elder

For those who want to wait for the pearly gates, go right ahead. It's like a modern-day person refusing to use electricity. All you have to do to access electricity is find an outlet, plug in an electronic device or appliance, and *voilà!* You get all sorts of cool stuff—toasted bread, music that's piped in from radio towers, movies and news, and fellow humans eating slugs on deserted islands.

We have to retrain ourselves to think of this energy force the same way we think of electricity. We don't wonder, *Am I good enough to plug my toaster oven into the outlet?* or *Have I prayed long enough or deep enough to deserve the right to flick on the kitchen lights?*

We don't feel guilty for wanting to turn on the radio and listen to NPR. The FP is just as nonprejudiced and available as electricity once we make the decision to really look for it.

And it's not that hard to find.

Anecdotal Evidence

> *"God is not the pushover that some people would like you to believe."*
>
> — ALEX FRANKOVITCH IN *SKINNY BONES*,
> BY BARBARA PARK

This is the section where we talk about the elephant in the room. Yes, I'm talking about God.

Unless you just crawled out from underneath a cabbage leaf, you've probably observed that an awful lot of people talk about this guy named God. One out of every seven days is devoted to worshipping him. Buildings of all shapes and sizes have been built to honor him. Many newspapers have a religious section right next to the political section, the local news, the weather, and the crossword puzzle.

Some version of "the dude" (to borrow a moniker from cult-classic *The Big Lebowski*) exists in every culture that has ever existed. Even physicists whose sole line of work is studying the properties and interactions of matter and energy know about the invisible force. Most of them do not call it God. Albert Einstein, for example, claimed no belief in the traditional God, but he sure as heck knew there was something a whole lot juicier out there in the cosmos. That juice, he said, was all he really cared about. The rest, he claimed, was just details.

The God most of us believe in is an invention of man, fabricated for the sake of convenience. We accept this human-made God as an indisputable fact. But it makes no sense. If God is love, if God is perfect, if God is all the other beneficent descriptions we ascribe to him, why would he toss anyone into a lion's den? Furthermore, why would anyone in their right mind want to hook up with a capricious and unjust god who gets his jollies from punishing them? Even the ditziest of women knows theoretically she shouldn't hang out with a guy who might hurt her.

I mean, who needs it?

God as Terrorist

"I don't know if God exists, but it would certainly be better for his reputation if he didn't."

— JULES RENARD, FRENCH AUTHOR

No sooner had I mastered my ABC's than I was taught that I, little Pammy Sue Grout, was a miserable sinner and had fallen short of the glory of God. It was a fact, same as two plus two equals four and *el-em-en-oh-pee* is more than one letter in the alphabetical lineup. The only redeeming part of this all-important lesson is at least I wasn't alone. Turns out, everybody else in the world is a sinner, too. Even Mrs. Beckwith, my tenderhearted kindergarten teacher who let me bring Pokey, my pet turtle, to class every other Monday.

The bad thing about being a sinner is it guarantees a one-way ticket to hell. It was a little hard getting a handle on hell, being I hadn't traveled much farther than the Kansas border. But, according to my dad, hell was not a place you wanted to be. It was hotter than my Aunt Gwen and Uncle Ted's house in Texas the summer their air conditioner broke. And, unlike that vacation that ended after four days, you stay in hell for eternity. To understand eternity, he said, you think of how you felt last December 26 waiting for Christmas again.

The escape clause is that you can "get saved."

So when I was four years old, with the church organist playing "Just as I Am," I walked to the front of the little Methodist church in Canton, Kansas, plopped down on my knobby little four-year-old knees, and asked the good Lord to "forgive me for my sins." My family, from a long line of Methodists, collectively breathed a sigh of relief. Dad and Mom called all the aunts and uncles that very night to broadcast the good news.

"Well, our oldest is officially saved now," they crowed proudly. "At least, we can be assured that Pam is going to heaven."

The best part, they figured, was that my conversion couldn't help but set a good example for my sister, Becki, who was two; and my brother, Bobby, who was only three months old, although I secretly hoped they would give him until he was old enough to talk.

Of course, you didn't want to take any chances. I mean, Jesus could come back at any time—night or day. He was like a thief in the night. He could come in the morning while you were stirring circles in your Cap'n Crunch cereal. He could come at recess while you were hanging from your knees on the monkey bars. He could even come at 2 in the morning while you were sleeping, which could be a real problem if you happened to be a heavy sleeper. Jesus could snatch you up before you had time to get the sleep out of your eyes.

And *that* you didn't even want to think about. I mean, Aunt Gwen and Uncle Ted's house was hot.

At the same time I was learning to accept my true sinful identity, I was being told over and over again that "God is love." Never mind that the churches presented God as a sort of hidden camera that watched over everything I did.

It made no rational sense. But, of course, I was only four. What did I know?

Even though I was yawningly close to being a perfect kid (I made straight A's, tried not to fight with my siblings, stayed away from drugs and alcohol, and even made my bed without being told), I felt I was constantly being critiqued by this "loving God" who was sitting up in heaven, gleefully rubbing his hands together whenever I screwed up. Which, gosh darn it (oops, there I go again, using his name in vain!) seemed to be pretty often.

What a legacy to dump on an innocent child.

God Looks Like Z.Z. Top and Other Annoying Myths

"Our ideas of God tells us more about ourselves than about Him."

— THOMAS MERTON, CHRISTIAN MYSTIC

Ask the average individual if he believes in God and he will probably say something like, "Well, duh!" However, it's unlikely he will have ever asked himself exactly what he means by God. When pressed, he'd probably offer some cliché about "the guy upstairs."

Trying to define God, of course, is impossible. God isn't static, any more than electricity or light is static. God lies beyond the material world of matter, shape, and form. It fills the cosmos, saturates reality, and supersedes time and space. But that doesn't stop us from trying to construct definitions. Here are the top eight whoppers we've made up about God:

Whopper #1: God is a him. Even though the progressive churches sometimes refer to God as *she,* the FP doesn't really have a gender. We certainly don't talk about Mrs. Electricity or Mr. Gravity. The more appropriate pronoun would be *it.* The FP is a force field that runs the universe, the same energy source that grows flowers, forms scabs over skinned knees, and constantly pushes for wholeness.

God is more like the force in *Star Wars,* a presence that dwells within us, a principle by which we live. That's why Luke Skywalker and Darth Vader have become such a phenomenon. *Star Wars* is a myth that speaks to us at a deep, gut level. Some part of us knows that "the force" is with us and that we, through our words, thoughts, and deeds, create the world.

Whopper #2: God looks like ZZ Top, makes black check marks after your name, and is basically too busy working on world hunger to care about you. God, if you believe the accepted box, is a little like Boo Radley in *To Kill a Mockingbird:* this mysterious neighbor constantly peering out the window of his penthouse suite, waiting to catch us doing something "naughty, naughty." We can't really see him, but we've been properly warned that he's there. Watching. Judging. Monitoring our every move. If you don't follow this commandment or if you break that rule, God just might send his angel Secret Service after you to bop you on the head like Little Bunny Foo-Foo.

Whopper #3: God plays favorites. The FP is a force field that's equally available to everyone. It's a natural capacity in all of us, not an exclusive gift bestowed upon a few. In fact, that is the primary lesson Jesus taught. God is within. You are part of God. You can perform miracles.

To worship Jesus the way we do is a little like worshipping Benjamin Franklin because he first discovered electricity. Ben Franklin sent that kite up in an electric storm so we could use the principle he demonstrated. He didn't do it so we'd build temples to him, paint pictures of him, and wear little commemorative keys around our necks. He wanted us to take the principle of electricity and use it—which we do to run radios and computers and air conditioners. Had we stopped with Ben's discovery the way we did with Jesus's discovery, we'd all be sitting in the dark.

Benjamin Franklin didn't invent electricity any more than Jesus invented spiritual principles. Lightning and the resulting electricity have always been available. We just didn't realize it or know how to access it. Galileo didn't invent gravity when he dropped the wooden ball off the leaning tower of Pisa. He just demonstrated it.

Likewise, Jesus demonstrated spiritual principles that he wants us to use and develop. We've wasted 2,000 years worshipping this idol of him instead of using the principles he taught us. Look through the Bible and nowhere does Jesus say, "Worship me." His call to us was "follow me." There's a big difference.

By making Jesus out to be a hero, we miss the whole point. Jesus wasn't saying, "I'm cool. Make statues of me; turn my birthday into a huge commercial holiday." He was saying, "Here, look what is possible. Look what we humans are capable of."

Jesus is our brother, our legacy, the guy we're supposed to emulate.

What Jesus was trying to tell us is that the churches, the religious leaders, and all their blaring rhetoric has drowned out God's truth. They've pulled the wool over our eyes by failing to mention the fact that the FP is not an object of worship, but a very real presence and a principle by which we should live.

Whopper #4: God rewards our suffering and gives brownie points for our sacrifice (better known as "Life sucks and then you die"). Many of us think life is some sort of boot camp for heaven. We believe this short life span is "only a test" for the paradise we're eventually going to earn. If we hang on and bear it, we'll someday walk through those pearly gates and be happy. These errors in thinking have been condensed into living facts. Nothing is plainer than the inevitability of sorrows and trials.

But what if it isn't necessary? What if there is no reason to be poor? Or get sick? Or do anything but live an abundant, exciting life? What if these tragic, difficult lives are another rumor made up by the churches and cemented into our consciousness by years and years of conditioning? What I'd like to suggest is that this heaven you're waiting for is available now. And that you've been sold a bill of goods about who you are and what is possible.

Whopper #5: God is just so demanding. The FP doesn't judge. It doesn't punish. It doesn't think, *Well, Sammy C. was a good boy yesterday, helping that little old lady cross the street. I think I'll answer his prayer about winning the* *lottery.* Those are thoughts Clarence Thomas might think. The FP doesn't need anything. It requires nothing of us. It makes no demands. It doesn't like Mother Teresa more than Celine Dion. Only misinformed humans, scrambling desperately to make sense of their world, came up with a God who plays eenie-meenie-minie-mo with our lives, a God who likes and dislikes the same people we do. Our fear has trapped us into a box that plays out our very limited perception.

Whopper #6: You don't want to ask too much from God; you certainly wouldn't want to bug him. As I've already pointed out, the FP is not a person; therefore you *cannot* bug him. The FP is a power, an unseen energetic force. It isn't finite or limited, so you certainly couldn't ask too much of it. As the old saying goes, you can take an eye-dropper or a bucket to the ocean. The ocean doesn't care. If anything, we don't use the FP power nearly enough. This is an all-powerful force we're talking about here, not some last-minute relief team that comes in to pay the mortgage. The FP is not an adversary that has to be coaxed to the bargaining table.

Whopper #7: God is just so vague. *Au contraire.* Once you get rid of the black cloud of rumors and half truths that hide your awareness, you'll find the unseen force communicates just as clearly as Dr. Phil. Once you rid yourself of the blocks, you'll be shown exactly what to do and how to do it.

Again, we need to condition ourselves to think of God more like we think of electricity. Electricity doesn't care who plugs in a curling iron. Electricity doesn't need proof we're good enough to make toast.

Whopper #8: God only answers when he's good and ready. There is never a time when God or "the force" isn't guiding you. And you do not have to wait for any green lights or "get out of jail free" cards. The big guy is available 24/7 once you're ready to focus your full attention on it. The FP's guidance happens (as they say about . . . well, something else)—through a song lyric on the radio, by a phone call from a long-lost friend. The trick is to pay attention, trust, and as I will continue to repeat, focus your full attention on it.

And while we're on the topic of God's will, let's get this out on the table. There is no place in our updated picture of God for a hell of everlasting torment or for a sadist who would or could attempt to put you there. Nor is there any room for the idea that sickness or deformity or death or poverty or limitation of any kind is the will of God. The will of God, for those who insist on using that term, is the ceaseless longing of the spirit in you to become all you're capable of being. Amen.

The Method

> *"Allowing myself to become a little nutty and irrational did open me up to certain mystical experiences."*
>
> — D. PATRICK MILLER,
> FOUNDER OF FEARLESS BOOKS

In this experiment, you're going to devote 48 hours to looking for evidence of this all-knowing, all-perfect FP. Call it God, if that feels more comfortable. Luckily, the FP exists every single place you could ever think to look.

To up the stakes, you're going to ask the FP for a blessing or what I call an unexpected gift. You're going to give it 48 hours to send you a gift you wouldn't normally receive—a surprise check in the mail, a card from an old friend, something that is truly unexpected. You don't get to specify the blessing (that comes later, in Experiment #4), but you do need to give a clearly defined request and a concrete deadline. And as always, it helps to ask for help in recognizing your gift.

When my friend Wendy tried this experiment, she received not just one but *two* unexpected blessings. She got a dollar-an-hour raise (her boss called out of the blue), and her brother who lives out-of-state and never calls unless there's a death in the family volunteered to help her move, something he's never done in the six moves she'd made before this one.

Robbin, another friend, went out to her car during the 48-hour time frame during which she was conducting the experiment and found a gorgeous, handmade leather purse, a gift left by a friend who had no idea she was doing the experiment.

"I love the purse so much, I still carry it today," she says.

Results, depending on your consciousness, vary. Some people get something simple. My friend Julie, for example, had a two-year-old boy she'd never seen before come sit beside her on a park bench. They smiled at each other like two reunited soul mates. Or it might be something pretty amazing. Another experimenter, Eric, was offered a free ski trip to Lake Tahoe.

Take note of how you feel about asking the energy field for a blessing. Do you feel a bit antsy, wonder if you're being selfish, doubt whether it's appropriate to ask for something good? This feeling provides telling insight. Maybe you don't believe you deserve a gift. That thought sends signals to the energy field and affects its resonance. Perhaps you think it's only appropriate to ask for something you need. That signal, too, is being radioed to the energy field.

To do this experiment properly, you have to set aside skepticism. Not forever; just for 48 short hours. All you have to do is spend two measly days expecting to see proof. Expect to see the dude in living color. Expect it with your whole heart. Expect it with every ounce of your soul. Like any good hypothesis, this one is falsifiable. If you don't hear from the FP in 48 hours, feel free to write it off.

1. Pick a time to start the experiment. "Now" usually works for me.

2. Jot down the time and the date.

3. Ask the FP to make its presence known. Ask for a blessing. If you like, repeat the "intention" or "approach" listed on the following lab report sheet. Or make up your own.

That's it. Let go. And observe.

∷　∷　∷

Lab Report Sheet

The Principle: The Dude Abides Principle

The Theory: There is an invisible energy force or field of infinite possibilities. And it's yours for the asking.

The Question: Does the FP exist?

The Hypothesis: If there's a 24/7 energy force equally available to everyone, I can access it at any time simply by paying attention. Furthermore, if I ask the force for a blessing, giving it a specific time frame and clear instructions, it'll send me a gift and say, "My pleasure."

Time Required: 48 hours

Today's Date: _11/30_ **Time:** _9 am pac_

Deadline for Receiving Gift: _12/2 9 am PC_

The Approach: I hate to break it to ya, FP, but folks are starting to talk. They're starting to wonder, "Is this guy for real?" I mean, really, like it'd be so much skin off your chin to come down here and call off this crazy hide-and-seek thing you've been playing. I'm giving you exactly 48 hours to make your presence known. I want a thumbs-up, a clear sign, something that cannot be written off as coincidence.

Research Notes: _____

_____

⁞⁞ ⁞⁞ ⁞⁞

"We now have a science of spirituality that is fully verifiable and objective."

— AMIT GOSWAMI, PH.D.,
RETIRED THEORETICAL PHYSICIST

EXPERIMENT #2

THE VOLKSWAGEN JETTA PRINCIPLE:

You Impact the Field and Draw from It According to Your Beliefs and Expectations

"Miracles are like pimples, because once you start looking for them you find more than you ever dreamed you'd see."

— LEMONY SNICKET (AKA DANIEL HANDLER)
IN *A SERIES OF UNFORTUNATE EVENTS*

The Premise

What shows up in our lives is a direct reflection of our inner thoughts and emotions. My friend Linda told me an amazing story about a young woman she once observed at the airport. This poor young thing was struggling with three heavy bags. But worse than the unwieldiness of her baggage was her less-than-positive attitude. With great gusto, she was vocalizing her immense disgust at a lack of help.

"Why," she kept shouting, "is the bus taking so long? Where in the hell is that bus? This is completely unacceptable!"

Linda said she might have felt sorry for the girl except that the very bus she was criticizing was five feet in front of her with its door wide open. Twice the bus circled, each time stopping to pick up passengers, but the irate young woman could not see it. The bus, thanks to her intense commitment to struggle and anger, was literally out of her energetic sphere.

That's why I named this principle after a popular model of car. Once a new model or make or brand enters your sphere of awareness, you suddenly notice it everywhere.

And that's what happens when we devote our minds to things we do not want.

Lack, unhappiness, and danger are no more prevalent than a Volkswagen Jetta, but once we bring them into our consciousness, they sadly take over.

According to physicists, there's a zero-point field (what I call the field of potentiality or the FP) where every possibility exists. For example, there's the possibility you could be a ballerina, another that you could be a U.S. senator. Still another possibility is being a bag lady in Haight-Ashbury. When it comes to the FP, the possibilities are infinite.

Since I'm not a physicist and can barely pronounce the name David Bohm, let alone understand his theory of layered realities, I prefer to think of the field as a gigantic Walmart with hundreds of thousands of "products," or possibilities. This is probably a good time to mention I'm not a fan of Walmart, that I've never quite been able to forgive the corporate giant for running my favorite corner pharmacy and fabric store out of business. But as a single mom on a budget, I do occasionally lower myself to shop there. And when I do, I know just where to find the fabric, the puzzles, the kids' shoes—all things I've been known to purchase. But I'm completely oblivious to most of the hundreds of thousands of products on the shelves.

Why? Because they're not what I'm looking for.

That doesn't mean they're not there. Doesn't mean they're not as "real" as the puzzles and shoes. It just means I'm not aware of them. For example, my daughter once came home from school with head lice. After panicking and briefly considering throwing myself off the nearest bridge, I finally concluded I would provide a much better parental example by going in search of lice shampoo. Sure enough, on an aisle at Walmart I'd walked down dozens, probably hundreds of times was a complete selection of lice shampoo. Why had I never noticed it before?

Because it wasn't what I was looking for.

The Chains That Bind Us

"Your wildest misperceptions, your weird imaginings, your blackest nightmares all mean nothing."

— A COURSE IN MIRACLES

A few years ago, a sweepstakes agency gave away 100 free trips, to anywhere winners wanted to go. That meant lucky winners could fly to Paris to see the Eiffel Tower or jet to Australia and climb Ayers Rock or lounge on a beach in the Caribbean islands. And you know what? Ninety-five percent of the winners picked a destination within four hours of their home. Four hours.

That pretty much sums up the human condition. So much is out there, but most of us choose to stay within four hours of our "comfort zones." We refuse to budge, even when there's ample evidence we're missing out on big things. Without being truly conscious of it, we spend the lion's share of our waking hours immersed in the comfort zone of negativity. The pull of the negative is so strong that many of us navigate our entire days jumping from one depressing thought to another: *I overslept again, This war is unconscionable, The economy is in shambles, Gas is expensive, My boss* [or *my kid* or *my _____*] *is driving me crazy.*

Negativity and fear start the minute we're born: "It's a scary world out there, Jimmy. Don't you dare talk to strangers. Don't you dare sing that silly song at the grocery store. Someone might hear."

We learn to limit. We learn to believe in scarcity. We learn that our natural inclination to love and to create and to dance is impractical and crazy.

Our parents think it's their sworn duty to teach us to be careful, to be responsible, to act like adults. And if for some reason we're lucky enough to get parents who don't dispense these lessons, our culture quickly indoctrinates us into believing that collecting material things is our purpose in life and that the only way to get those goodies is to put our proverbial noses to the grindstone. By the time we're in grade school, we're already masters at competition, old pros at living in scarcity and fear.

But guess what? It's all a big ruse, a bad habit. As *A Course in Miracles* clearly states, "Once you develop a thought system of any kind, you live by it and teach it."

Once you form a belief, you attach all your senses and all your life to its survival.

Physicists call this phenomenon "collapse of the wave." Infinite numbers of quantum particles are out in the universal field dancing around, spreading out in waves. The moment someone looks at these energy waves they solidify like gelatin in the refrigerator. Your observing is what makes them appear solid, real, material.

Remember in Disney's *Snow White* when she's lying on the forest floor crying? She feels as if all these eyes are staring at her. And indeed, dozens of forest creatures are skittering and scampering about. But the moment she raises her head to look, all the cute little birds, squirrels, and deer dive behind trees. All she can see is a solid, unmoving forest.

In reality, our universe is a moving, scampering energy field with infinite possibilities, but because our eyes have locked in on problem mode, that's what appears to be reality.

It Sure *Looks* Like Reality
(or You'll See It When You Believe It)

"You will not break loose until you realize that you yourself forge the chains that bind you."

— ARTEN IN *THE DISAPPEARANCE OF THE UNIVERSE,* BY GARY RENARD

In 1970, Colin Blakemore and G. F. Cooper, scientists at Cambridge University, did a fascinating experiment with kittens. This must have been before animal rights activists got vocal, because what they did was take a litter of kittens and deprive them of light. Except for once a day, for just an hour or two, when the scientists beamed in just enough light for the kittens to see a couple of vertical black and white stripes. That's it. A couple of hours, a couple of stripes. Now, I don't know whether their consciences finally got the better of them or whether some PETA-type predecessor started breathing down their necks, but after several months they released the kittens from the dark. What they discovered was the kittens' cortical cells (cells in the eyeball for those of you who aren't scientifically minded) that favored nonvertical orientation had gone into hibernation. They could no longer make out horizontal lines. They literally bumped into horizontal ropes that were stretched out in front of them.

In 1961, when anthropologist Colin Turnbull studied Pygmies, he took one of his subjects outside of the forest where he lived. Since he'd never been exposed to wide, open plains, the Pygmy's sense of depth did the same disappearing act as the kittens' cortical cells. Turnbull pointed out a herd of buffalo in the distance, and the Pygmy, whose depth perception was distorted, refused to believe it. "It *has* to be ants," he insisted.

His perceptions were influenced by what he had been conditioned to see. As thinking beings, we continually try to make sense of our world. Sounds like a good thing, right? Except that any piece of information that doesn't quite fit with our beliefs, we alter without even noticing. We knead and we squeeze until everything finally fits into the tight box of our limited belief system.

We think what we perceive with our senses is true, but the fact that I will keep banging you over the head with is . . . it's only one-half of one-millionth of a percent of what's possible.

At the base of the brain stem, about the size of a gumdrop, is a group of cells whose job is to sort and evaluate incoming data. This control center, known as the *reticular activating system* (RAS), has the job of sending what it thinks is urgent to the active part of the brain and to steer the nonurgent stuff to the back. But as it's organizing, it's also busy interpreting, drawing inferences, and filtering out anything that doesn't jibe with what we believe.

In other words, we rehearse ahead of time the world we want to see. Too bad we all picked up the wrong script.

This simple, 48-hour experiment will prove that what you see in life is none other than what you look for. It will also prove that it's possible to *find* anything you look for. And most important, it will prove that by changing what you look for, you can radically change what shows up in your world.

Anecdotal Evidence

> *"Toto, I don't think we're in Kansas anymore."*
>
> — BUMPER STICKER SEEN IN LAWRENCE, KANSAS

You've probably never heard of Peter and Eileen Caddy. But I'll bet the name Findhorn rings a bell. Remember that garden in Scotland that yielded cabbages big enough to knock over a postal truck? Well, Peter and Eileen Caddy are the folks who grew those 40-pound cabbages (keep in mind that the average cabbage is four pounds, five ounces), and they did it by focusing their thoughts on a higher truth.

They certainly didn't have anything else going for them. In fact, when the Caddys, their three sons, and fellow spiritual seeker Dorothy Maclean moved into the trailer on that windblown peninsula jutting out into the North Sea, the land could best be described as dead and profitless. Nobody in their right mind would have chosen it as a spot to grow anything, let alone a garden. The soil—if you could call it that—consisted of rocks and sand, the gales were strong enough to knock over the average second grader, and their "less than *Better Homes*" locale was smack-dab between a garbage dump and a dilapidated garage.

But by focusing on a higher truth, they created a garden that can only be described as miraculous. Although it was the 40-pound cabbages that got all the publicity, the Caddys also grew 65 other types of vegetables, 21 kinds of fruits, and 42 different herbs. And this is before they started adding flowers.

I know what you're thinking: rich compost and good organic husbandry. But the truth is, the Caddys' soil was so pathetic that the county extension agent said even compost couldn't help. At the time they started their experiment in higher consciousness, the Caddys had never gardened, nor did they have money to invest in gardening supplies. They were broke—to put it mildly. Peter, who had managed a successful four-star hotel, had been laid off, and the six of them were living on unemployment that amounted to roughly $20 a week.

No, they started growing vegetables for one reason: they thought it might be a nice gesture to feed their three growing boys. But as they began aligning their consciousness with spiritual truth and nothing else, all sorts of strange things started happening. Straw bales fell off passing trucks just in time to mulch. Leftover bags of cement mix mysteriously showed up in a neighbor's trash bin just in time to pour a patio. Their plants, while the crops of their neighbors suffered, became resistant to diseases and pests. Eventually, people started flocking to the Caddys' garden, and today Findhorn is a prosperous spiritual community that attracts 14,000 seekers every year.

As Peter says, "You can bring about anything by your thoughts. Align yourself with God consciousness and you can bring about truth in material form. What you think, you create."

There is no power on Earth that can cut you off from this source except your own consciousness.

The Method

"Everything we think we're seeing is all just a guess, a prediction our brains are making."

— KURT ANDERSON, AUTHOR OF *TRUE BELIEVERS*

For the next 48 hours (that's all—a pain-free, two-day commitment; you are free to go back to your miserable life as soon as this experiment is over), you are going to actively look for certain things. And just like sixth graders who start out dissecting worms, not human bodies, you're going to begin with something simple—green cars. Or if you insist, pick another color. Sunset beige, for example. For the first 24 hours of the experiment, you're going to make the following conscious intention. "I hereby intend, for the next day of my life, to look for [okay, you win] sunset-beige vehicles." Again, nothing special is required. Just keep your eyes open and make the intention. And then simply notice if your conscious awareness has made a difference in the number of sunset-beige cars you see.

On day two, during the second 24-hour period, you're going to make the intention to find yellow butterflies. Or purple feathers. Just make the intention. My friend Jeanette tried the experiment in January in the upper peninsula of Michigan and found yellow butterflies on stationery and on a paper cup at her daughter's friend's birthday party.

Another friend, Angela, was reading *The Secret* on a plane. This popular book on the universal law of attraction suggested that readers make an intention to receive a free cup of coffee. She laughed because, after all, the onboard flight attendant was just two aisles away from asking her that important flight-attendant question: "Coffee, tea, or soda?"

"That isn't quite fair," she noted, making the intention and moving on to the next paragraph.

But during her layover, a stranger who was sitting near her in the waiting lounge leaned over and said, "My flight was just called. I can't carry anything else. I haven't even taken a sip. Do you want this?"

You guessed it—it was a just-brewed Starbucks latte.

Lab Report Sheet

The Principle: The Volkswagen Jetta Principle

The Theory: You impact the field and draw from it according to your beliefs and expectations.

The Question: Do I really see only what I expect to see?

The Hypothesis: If I decide to look for sunset-beige cars and butterflies (or purple feathers), I will find them.

Time Required: 48 hours

Today's Date: _____ **Time:** _____

The Approach: According to this crazy Pam Grout girl, the world out there reflects what I want to see. She says that it's nothing but my own illusions that keep me from experiencing peace, joy, and love. So even though I suspect she's cracked, today I'm going to look for sunset-beige cars. Tomorrow, I'll go butterfly hunting.

a. Number of sunset-beige cars observed: _____

b. Number of butterflies observed: _____

Research Notes: _____

_____

⠶ ⠶ ⠶

"Miracles do not happen in contradiction to nature, but only in contradiction to what is known in nature."

— St. Augustine,
Latin philosopher and theologian

51

EXPERIMENT #3

THE ALBY EINSTEIN PRINCIPLE:

You, Too, Are a Field of Energy

*"It's right underneath your fingers, baby.
That's all you have to understand—everything is
right underneath your fingers."*

— RAY CHARLES, AMERICAN SINGER AND PIANIST

The Premise

I'm not going to bore you with an entire text on quantum physics. I've read dozens, and believe me, they're not pretty. But there are a couple of rumors going around that must be quashed before we go any further.

For starters, who you think you are is not who you really are.

You think you have a limited life—something like 70 or 80 years—and then you wrinkle up, get rheumatism, and keel over. *Ka-boom!* It's all over. But this isn't any more true than that dream you had last night about the tall blonde.

Your body is an impostor, a tiny fraction of who you really are. Ninety-nine percent of who you are is invisible and untouchable. This body that I think is Pam Grout—this skinny 5'10" woman with perpetual complexion problems—is just a speck of who I really am, no more the real me than those two-month-old baby pictures where I'm wearing the embarrassing pink bonnet.

Don't feel bad if you've fallen for the trap that you, your body, and the world around you are nothing but matter. It's not easy standing on the brink of a revolution. These new ideas that scientists are finally starting to take seriously are challenging everything we believe about how our world works and how we define ourselves.

The Whole Truth and Nothing But the Truth

"Everything you know about the universe and its laws is more than likely to be 99.99 percent wrong."

— FRED ALAN WOLF, PH.D., AMERICAN QUANTUM PHYSICIST

What Einstein discovered and what that famous equation $E = mc^2$ means is that mass and energy are basically two forms of the same thing. Energy is liberated matter, and matter is energy waiting to happen.

There is a huge amount of energy—a preposterously huge amount—trapped in every living thing. You, making the assumption that you're an average-size human being, contain no less than 7 times 10 to the 18th (7×10^{18}) joules of potential energy. That may not mean much to you now, but let's pretend you want to make a point. If you were a bit more cunning and knew how to liberate this energy, you could use it to explode yourself with the force of 30 very large hydrogen bombs.

In other words, the material world is nothing but dense energy patterns. Scientists put all these sub-subatomic particles into a particle accelerator, collided them, and ultimately discovered that there is no particle at the source. It's all just pure unbounded energy vibrating so fast that it defies measurement and observation. So, despite how it looks to the naked eye, you are energy.

In fact, nothing in the world is actually solid. Not you, not this book, not the chair you're sitting on. Break the solid world down to its tiniest components and you'll find dancing particles and empty space. It only looks solid because the energy is vibrating a little slower than the speed of light.

That's what energy is—vibrating particles. That means you, this book, and the chair are actually vibrating.

Energy is a pretty nebulous thing. You can't see it, scratch it, or take it out to dinner. But you can (and do every day) influence how it flows through you. And since it's the building block of everything in the universe, that's a powerful thing.

Try this experiment that I learned from energy pioneer Donna Eden.

1. Bring your palms toward each other, like you're about to clap, but stop three inches before your hands make contact.

2. Now twist your wrists so your arms form an X. The wrists should be at the center of the X and still three inches apart.

3. Draw your attention to the space between your wrists. Because your wrists contain several energy centers, the energies will connect and, most likely, you will feel some sensation in the area between them.

4. Try moving your wrists about an inch closer and then out a few inches back and forth.

See? What did I tell you? You're energy. At each moment, you mold and shape this energy by your consciousness. You do so with every thought, every intention, every action. How you feel; what you think, believe, and value; and how you live your life affect how the energy flows through you. To put it in simplest terms, this affects how you vibrate.

And how you vibrate affects what you pull in from the interlocking, interbalancing, ever-moving energy field in which you swim. You pull out of this field and into your world anything that happens to be vibrating on the same frequency or wavelength.

Let's say you're feeling excited, joyful, and grateful. Those emotions send out high-frequency vibrations that magnetize more things to be excited, joyful, and grateful about. Anything with the same high frequency will prance on over to your energy field.

However, if you're scared, guilt-ridden, and convinced there's a terrorist around every corner, you're sending out low-frequency vibrations that will attract ugly things into your life.

We always attract our vibrational match. We are the initiators of the vibrations, and therefore the "magnets," or the cause.

It works the same way as a tuning fork. Ding a tuning fork in a room filled with tuning forks that are calibrated to different pitches, and only the ones calibrated to the same frequency will ding, too. And they'll ding all the way across the Minneapolis Metrodome. Like forces attract: it's a classic rule of physics.

There Is No "You" and "Them"

*"Anyone who is not shocked by physics
has not understood it."*

— NIELS BOHR, DANISH PHYSICIST

As if you didn't already have enough weirdness to contend with, I'm going to throw in one more tiny detail. Everything in the physical world as we know it is connected to every other thing in the physical world. You are attached and engaged to one underlying universal energy field. "The field," as Daddy Alby Einstein said, "is the only reality."

Things appear separate because they're vibrating at different wavelengths, just as the note C vibrates at a different wavelength than B-flat. Each of these vibrations creates a strand in the electromagnetic field, which in turn instructs energy where to go and what to do.

This pulsating energy field is the central engine of your being and your consciousness. Where is this field? Well, there's no place it's *not*. Everything in the universe is hooked up to the energy field—all life forms, whether African zebras, the hostas in your garden, or those melting icebergs. Your intelligence, creativity, and imagination interact with this magnificent and complex energy field.

We may look like separate bodies with separate ideas, but we are all just one big pulsating, vibrating field of consciousness.

Anecdotal Evidence

"It ain't what you don't know that gets you into trouble. It's what you know for sure that just ain't so."

— Mark Twain, American author

Edwene Gaines is one of my favorite Unity ministers. She's funny, she's wise, and she knows how spiritual principles work. She travels throughout the U.S. giving prosperity seminars in which she teaches people how to live more abundant, God-centered lives.

But like the rest of us, Edwene had to learn about spiritual principles through trial and error. She tells a hilarious story about her "first big demonstration." A *demonstration,* according to Unitics (that is, folks who hang out at Unity churches), is when you pull something you want or need out of thin air—more or less.

At the time of Edwene's first demonstration, she was relatively new to spiritual principles. She was what you could politely call broke. As she says, "I didn't have two dimes to rub together."

But she heard this crazy rumor from her spiritual teacher that not only did God like her, but he wanted to open the gates of heaven and pour out his blessings—if she simply learned how to direct her energy. But first she had to know what she wanted and when she wanted it.

That was easy. Within 15 minutes Edwene filled a whole yellow legal pad with her desires—new green shoes, a new male partner, a new car, and so on.

She decided she also wanted a week's vacation to Mexico City. She'd never been there, but she figured it would be a great place to practice her Spanish. Plus she'd always wanted to see the Pyramid of the Sun, the Pyramid of the Moon, and Diego Rivera's paintings.

Edwene didn't have any money for the trip, so writing it down was, as she put it, a "bit of a joke." But she figured, *What the heck!* She even went down to a travel agent, looked at brochures, and made a tentative reservation three months in advance of the date she decided she wanted to travel.

"I figured the worst that could happen is I'd be embarrassed in front of the travel agent when I wasn't able to pay," Edwene explained.

"That's only because you don't feel rich," her teacher said. "You're not vibrating as a rich person."

"Well, I could have told you that," Edwene replied. "Have you had a look at my checking account lately? I'm having trouble paying my electric bill."

"That's why you need to go out and do something to make yourself feel rich," her teacher insisted.

Edwene decided her biggest challenge was the grocery store.

"I was one of those people who bought the bare minimum—beans, cornbread, flour, the basics," she says. "I didn't dare splurge on any of that foo-foo stuff. Nothing like bubble bath. I had a budget."

So the next time she was at the grocery store, she decided to saunter over to the gourmet counter, just for a gander.

She noticed a bottle of olives stuffed with almonds. She took one look at that and just knew that was what rich people ate. So she bought it, took her groceries home, and called her friend Lana.

"Lana, I'm coming over. We're going to sit by your pool, and we're going to get out your new crystal wineglasses and drink that bottle of wine you just bought. We're going to eat the olives I just splurged on, and we're going to pretend we're on an exotic vacation in Mexico City."

"Say what?" Lana said.

She eventually agreed to play along. And sure enough, they sat by Lana's pool, drinking wine, eating olives, laughing, and pretending to be vacationing in Mexico City.

"Well, darling, which pyramid should we visit tomorrow?" Edwene would ask. "Or maybe you'd rather go to the beach."

And then Lana would answer, "Let's do both, and after that we can walk through the marketplace and listen to mariachis."

They had so much fun that Lana decided she wanted to go to Mexico City, too. The next day, she went down to the same travel agency and made her reservations.

Within a week, Lana's mom called her and said, "Hey, guess what? I'd like to pay for that ticket to Mexico City."

"And *I* was the one doing the affirmations," Edwene now jokes.

A few weeks later, the travel agent called Edwene and informed her that unless she came down to pay for her tickets that day, she was going to have to let them go.

"Okay, I'll be right there," Edwene said to the travel agent, even though she felt like Old Mother Hubbard with the completely bare cupboards. She got in her car and decided it was time she had a severe talking-to with God.

"God," she said, "now, I've done everything I know how to do here. I've made my list. I've done my affirmations. I've been acting rich. The way I figure it, the rest is up to you. And, Big Guy, since this travel agent is calling, I'm going to go ahead and go on down, and that money better be there."

On the way to the travel agency, she got a hunch to stop by her mom's house.

"Now I know myself well enough to know that I was probably thinking that if I told my mom about Lana's mom buying her ticket, maybe she'd agree to buy my ticket," Edwene admits.

She went into her mom's house, acted just as sweet as can be, and told her mom about this vacation she and Lana had cooked up. She finished her story, looked up at her mom, and said, "And you know what? Lana's mom even agreed to pay for Lana's ticket. Isn't that wonderful?"

"That *is* wonderful," Edwene's mom said. "What are you going to do?"

Discouraged, Edwene concluded her visit and started to walk out the door when her mom asked if she'd be kind enough to run out and get her mail.

Her mom's house had a long driveway, so Edwene walked out to the mailbox, kicking at stones and cursing under her breath. On the way back, Edwene decided to take a little look-see through the mail. She noticed a letter addressed to her.

"Now understand, I hadn't lived at my mom's house for 15 years and hadn't received mail there for 15 years," she says.

Edwene, not having a clue who this person on the return address was, ripped open the envelope. Lo and behold, there was a letter from an old roommate who had gotten married since she and Edwene had lived together 15 years earlier. At the time, they were both young, poor, and forced to decorate with what Edwene calls "early Salvation Army."

Not three months after they moved in together, Edwene landed a job teaching overseas and left the roommate, the apartment, and the used furniture behind.

Here's what the letter said:

> *Dear Edwene: I was looking through the Houston phone book the other day and saw your parents' address. I wanted to tell you that I've gotten married and moved into a nice new house with my husband. We furnished our house with new furniture, so I sold all that furniture we bought 15 years ago. Turns out—would you believe it?—that some of it was pretty valuable. I didn't feel right keeping all the money since we had worked so hard to furnish that place. Please find a check for your half of the money.*

"And do you know?" says Edwene. "It was exact amount I needed to pay for my ticket, to the penny, plus $100 for spending money."

Edwene also added a funny sequel to her story. Sure enough, Lana and Edwene had a marvelous time in Mexico City. They shopped, sat by the pool, visited pyramids, and strolled through the markets.

"And everywhere we went, Lana got flowers," Edwene says. "We'd be walking through the marketplace, and the mariachis would stop playing and bring Lana a gardenia. One day, we were on the bus and this guy jumps on, hands Lana a rose, and jumps off. One night at supper, this big white box arrives at our table. Lana opens it up and it's a dozen orchids.

"By this time, I'm starting to feel left out. I say to God, 'Look, buddy, I need a sign that I'm loved, too,'" Edwene says.

Not 15 minutes later, the waiter at the restaurant brought over the hors d'oeuvres.

"And that God has such a sense of humor," Edwene laughs. "Do you know what that waiter brought? Olives stuffed with almonds."

The Method

"The Western scientific community, and actually all of us, are in a difficult spot, because in order to maintain our current mode of being, we must ignore a tremendous amount of information."

— CLEVE BACKSTER,
PLANT RESEARCHER AND FORMER CIA AGENT

Even though this principle is one of the cornerstone spiritual principles (remember, *spiritual* just means the opposite of *material*), it actually first came to light not in a church, but in a physics lab. Yes, it was scientists who first discovered that, despite all appearances to the contrary, human beings are not matter, but continually moving waves of energy.

In this experiment you're going to prove that your thoughts and feelings also create energy waves. Here's what you do: Get two wire coat hangers, easy to obtain in most any closet. Untwist the neck of each hanger until you've got just two straight wires. These are your "Einstein wands." Or rather they *will* be when you shape them into an L, about 12 inches long for the main part and 5 inches for the handle. Cut a plastic straw in half (you can score one free of charge at any McDonald's), slide the handle that you just bent inside the straws (it'll make your wands swing

63

easily), and bend the bottom of the hanger to hold the straw in place.

Now, pretend you're a double-fisted, gun-slinging Matt Dillon from *Gunsmoke* with the wands held chest high and about ten inches from your body. They'll flap all over the place at first (like I said, you're an ongoing river of energy), so give them a few moments to settle down. Once they've stopped flapping, you're ready to begin the experiment.

With your eyes straight ahead, vividly recall some very unpleasant event from your past. Depending on the intensity of your emotion, the wands will either stay straight ahead (weak intensity) or will point inward, tip to tip. The wands are following the electromagnetic bands around your body, which have contracted as a result of the negative frequency generated by your unpleasant thought and emotions.

Now make your frequencies turn positive by thinking about something loving or joyous. The wands will now expand outward as your energy field expands to your positive energy flow.

Okay, now keep your eyes straight ahead, but focus your attention on an object to your far right or far left and watch your wands follow your thoughts. The more you play with this, the more adept you'll become at feeling the vibrational shift as you change from one frequency to another.

Lab Report Sheet

The Principle: The Alby Einstein Principle

The Theory: You are a field of energy in an even bigger field of energy.

The Question: Could it be true that I'm made up of energy?

The Hypothesis: If I am energy, I can direct my energy.

Time Required: Two hours of experimentation.

Today's Date: _____ **Time:** _____

The Approach: Wahoo, baby! With nothing but my powerful thoughts and energy, I can make these wands rock and roll. Just think what other magic I can undoubtedly do. As a famous president once said, "Bring it on."

Research Notes: _____

_____

⠿　⠿　⠿

"To be a true explorer in science—to follow the unprejudiced lead of pure scientific inquiry—is to be unafraid to propose the unthinkable, and to prove friends, colleagues, and scientific paradigms wrong."

— LYNNE MCTAGGART, AUTHOR OF *THE FIELD*

EXPERIMENT #4

THE ABRACADABRA PRINCIPLE:

Whatever You Focus on Expands

"I can manipulate the external influences in my life as surely as I can make a baby cry by grinning."
— AUGUSTEN BURROUGHS, AMERICAN AUTHOR

The Premise

When I first heard my thoughts could bring material goods into my life, I did what any intelligent, thinking person would do. I scoffed. But I also decided to give it a try. What could it hurt to conduct a secret experiment?

Andrea, my teacher, said to write down three things I wanted. That's all. I didn't have to zap them out of thin air.

I didn't have to work out a budget. I just had to make a list. What the heck. *I want a bicycle, a computer, and a piano.*

Within two weeks, I was the proud owner of a beautiful red mountain bike and an IBM PC Junior. The piano took a little bit longer. But some years ago, my friend Wendy, who was moving to Maryland, called and told me that if I'd come get it, I could have her beautiful cherrywood Kimball. My daughter, forced to take piano lessons, has been cursing me ever since.

Yes, this is the chapter you've all been waiting for: The chapter on how to manifest material things. It's the spiritual principle that attracts would-be believers like 15-year-old males to Megan Fox.

Let me guess. At some point in your life, you've read *Think and Grow Rich, The Magic of Believing, The Power of Positive Thinking,* or some combination thereof. As old and crotchety as these books might be, there's a reason they're still in print. They speak of a universal truth. *If you know what you want, you can have it.*

My friend Chris—okay, most of my friends—think this principle employs magic, some mysterious juju that might work for some people but not others. But it's not any more complicated than walking from Biloxi, Mississippi, to New Orleans once you have the right map. Let's say Biloxi is what you have now—a beat-up '94 Escort, a job you can't stand, and a lot of weekends watching DVDs by yourself. New Orleans, where you really want to be, is a shiny new Jaguar, a high-paying job that utilizes and appreciates your greatest strengths, and weekends watching movies with an astoundingly hot specimen of the opposite sex.

So, how do you get there? You start focusing on New Orleans. You forget that Biloxi and your beat-up '94 Escort even exist. And you remember that at every moment, you're either heading toward New Orleans or you're doubling back toward Biloxi. Every thought is a step in one direction or the other. Thoughts that take you back to Biloxi are *Good jobs and hot dates are not that available,* or the even more popular *Good jobs and hot dates are available, but not for the likes of me.*

Thoughts that move you toward New Orleans go something like this: *That new job is going to be so amazing,* and *Man, is this person sitting next to me on my couch ever so fine.* The more energy and excitement you invest, the quicker you'll get there.

Some people get stirred up, take a few steps toward their desires, panic, and turn right back around toward Biloxi. Others leave the Biloxi city limits, walk for a while, take a rest to look around, and then get pissed because it doesn't look like New Orleans.

Of course it doesn't look like New Orleans. You're not there yet. You're still seeing countryside that's just outside Biloxi, stuff you're going to have to pass through to get to New Orleans. But you've left Biloxi. Say a cheer and keep focusing. Whatever you do, don't stop walking. The only way to reach the sweet, champagne-drenched finish line of where you want to be is to keep your nose pointed in that direction. Do not turn around and look back. Biloxi is history. Stay focused on . . . did I mention New Orleans?

At first, you'll feel glorious about this new heroic endeavor. You'll be astonished by how easy it is for you to stay focused on the beautiful city of New Orleans. You'll be laughing and skipping and enjoying the vistas. But, inevitably, the menacing distractions will crop up. Your thoughts will get sore, they'll get bored with the new routine, and they'll want to head back toward Biloxi—you know, just for a quick visit, just for one cup of tea. You start spending less and less time on New Orleans and more and more time on why the whole endeavor is futile. Maybe you should put it out of its misery before it's old enough to remember where you live.

But don't do that. Just keep walking, keep focusing on New Orleans.

At the risk of appearing anal, I want to make it clear that the Biloxi–New Orleans example is only a metaphor. And the last thing I'd ever want to do is offend Biloxi, which happens to be a really cool town with the nearly new Frank Gehry–designed Ohr-O'Keefe Museum of Art. The big thing to remember is there's no real physical work involved. It's all about training your mind, that incorrigible slacker.

It sounds like pie in the sky, I know. But I've seen it happen time and time again. Getting to New Orleans doesn't take any particular gift. It just takes a willingness to keep walking. And focusing your attention, energy, and awareness.

I always think of a magician pulling a scarf through a hole. If you can just grab ahold of one tiny end, you can pull it all the way through. That's all it takes—one itty-bitty end. Decide you want it and keep focusing until you've pulled it all the way through.

What can you manifest? Pretty much anything you've ever seen, heard, or experienced. The world is basically your own mail-order catalog. If you've seen it, or even if you can imagine it, just grab an end of that scarf and start walking.

Maybe I should be more specific. My friend Don's "New Orleans" was a Martin guitar. Martin guitars start at $1,100, and while he didn't have the ready cash, Don made the intention to own a Martin guitar. He didn't do a damned thing, just kept believing (focusing on that guitar) that someday, somehow he'd get one.

Nearly a year later, he got a message from his mom: "Your dad just picked up an old guitar at a garage sale for $5. It can be a toy for Daisy."

Well, that old toy for Don's daughter Daisy was a rare 1943 Martin 000-28, one of only 100 made—the same guitar Eric Clapton plays—worth somewhere in the neighborhood of $20,000. It seems that Daisy will have to wait and inherit the guitar in Don's will.

I like to call this the Statue of Liberty principle. Even though this principle is the beacon that represents everything people think they want—vacations to Jamaica, a big home in Malibu—it's actually way down on Maslow's hierarchy of needs. It's only on the first, maybe second rung. You need to get this principle down, of course, so you can take your mind off material worries, and so that you can know the truth about who you are, but none of this "stuff" is what you *really* want. Not really.

Jesus could never have brought Lazarus back to life and multiplied all those fishes and loaves if he'd been preoccupied by the desire for a beachside residence. That said, I do not want to make you feel guilty for wanting a big home in Malibu. There is not one thing wrong with a big home in Malibu. Or anything else you want. Do not feel guilty. Want it. Walk toward it with all your heart and might. Just know there are higher rungs. And that most people hoard material things out of fear. And fear, after all, is what we're attempting to move away from.

Lining Up Your Ducks
(or What Coherence Is)

*"Great spirit is everywhere. It is not necessary to speak to
him in a loud voice. He hears whatever is
in our minds and hearts."*

— BLACK ELK, LAKOTA MEDICINE MAN

Most people think they can incite change only by
addressing God with some screech for "HELP!" But since we
now know God is the force field that runs the universe,
we also know *every* thought incites change. Every time we
think anything—be it a silent *That skirt makes her look like
John Travolta in Hairspray* or *I'll commit hari-kari if I don't
get that raise*—we influence the field of infinite potentiality.
I think I should probably repeat that *every single thought
affects the FP.*

The only reason we don't change water into wine or
heal cancer with one touch is because our thoughts are
scattered all over the place. Instead of being one, constant,
well-aimed tuning fork, our thoughts are more like a junior
high band of beginning trumpet players.

On one hand, we pray for things to work out, but on the
other, we worry they won't. At the same time we imagine a
positive outcome, we secretly think optimism is a bunch of
baloney. We want to be committed to a relationship with
so-and-so, but what if he leaves? We want to make money,
but didn't the Bible say something about camels and rich
people and the eye of a needle?

The force is literally bouncing off walls. *Go this way. No,
wait; go that way.* It's knocking around like a lightning bug
in a Mason jar. It's being dissipated because we have no
clear bead on what we really want. It's not that the field of

potentiality isn't answering our prayers. It's just that we're "praying" for too many things.

When you figure the average person has something like 60,000 thoughts a day, you come to realize that your life is being "prayed" about by a heck of a lot more than the "Please, God, let me get out of this speeding ticket" you uttered when you first noticed the flashing red lights.

Sure, you begged for peace of mind today, but you also spent 1,200 thoughts obsessing about that damned co-worker who stole your website idea. Yes, you made the intention to "think and grow rich," but you also devoted 500 thoughts to worrying about your overdue car payment. When you understand prayer for what it really is, it's easier to understand why that one-time plea to God doesn't always pan out.

The only reason Jesus could walk on water was because 100 percent of his thoughts (prayers) believed he could. He had overcome the world's thought system that says *Only an idiot would be stupid enough to step out of the boat.* There was not one doubt—not a single thought (prayer) in his consciousness that didn't fully believe it.

Your mind is very powerful, no matter how badly you disrespect the privilege, no matter how ineffectual you feel. Every single thought produces form at some level. Just because those thoughts are screwed up (and believe me, if you're a human, at least some of your thoughts are screwed up) doesn't make them weak or ineffective. Weak and ineffective at getting what you want, maybe, but never weak and ineffective.

Newton's First Law of Prayer

"By choosing your thoughts, and by selecting which emotional currents you will release and which you will reinforce, you determine the . . . effects that you will have upon others, and the nature of the experiences of your life.

— GARY ZUKAV, AUTHOR OF *SEAT OF THE SOUL*

When you throw a tennis ball in the air, you can count on it coming down. Granted, it might fall in the neighbor's petunias or on the roof of the 7-Eleven, where you'll need a ladder to retrieve it, but it's guaranteed to come back down.

Intention is just like that tennis ball. It comes back just the way you send it out. Like Newton said in his famous third law of motion, for every action there is an equal and opposite reaction. What you give out, what you "pray" about . . . you get back in equal measure. If you send out thoughts of fear, you get back things to be scared of. If you lie, you'll be lied to. If you criticize, you get criticized. But if you send out love, you get big, bounteous love back. If you send out blessings, you get blessed in turn.

If you want to know what you're really "praying" for, take a look around your life. You'll see your innermost thoughts, the real desires of your heart, the prayers no one knows about but you.

A friend of mine was fearful of spiders. She used to worry that she'd reach into her makeup drawer some morning and instead of grabbing a lipstick, she'd find her hands wrapped around a giant spider. This unfounded thought passed through her brain every morning for months until . . . guess what? She reached into her makeup drawer and grabbed a big, fat, hairy wolf spider.

To put it another way, thought is creative. The thoughts you hold in your mind, both conscious and unconscious, create what you see in your life. Every thought has a certain vibration. It boomerangs back to you according to its pitch, intensity, and depth of feeling. Your thoughts show up in your life in proportion with their constancy, intensity, and power.

Shoot-out at the I'm O.K., You're O.K. Corral (or How Your Mind Works)

"I am crowded inside."

— PRADEEP VENUGOPAL, INDIAN BLOGGER

Your mind is engaged in an ongoing showdown between different, conflicting parts of yourself. These splintered intentions, if you will, set all sorts of dynamics into motion. Let's say you have a conscious intention to buy a new house. At the same time you set that intention into motion, you simultaneously send out an unconscious but equally potent fear of a higher mortgage payment. You start fretting about interest rates, and worrying about the termite contract you inadvertently let expire on your current house—both of which send out even more unconscious intentions. If these unconscious fear intentions are stronger than the conscious desire intentions . . . well, guess which one wins?

The dynamic of opposing intentions can produce confusion and doubt. As you become open to new perceptions and desires and simultaneously experience fear and anguish, you set up a struggle.

If it keeps up, you start to doubt that setting intentions even works. Or at least you conclude it doesn't work for *you*. You become discouraged and start believing that life and circumstances are more powerful than you are.

Believe me, they're not. Not even close. Your conflicting intentions are simply creating turbulence in the field of potentiality.

Your thoughts are extremely powerful. But the FP doesn't respond only to your pleas. Let me repeat: it responds to *every* thought—conscious and unconscious—with opposing sides battling it out. Here are four of the most common battlefields:

1. **The rut.** We humans have this annoying tendency to fall into habitual patterns. Remember those 60,000 daily thoughts I mentioned earlier? Well, all but 1,000 of those thoughts are the exact same thoughts you had yesterday. Scientists tell us that 98 percent of our 60,000 thoughts are repeats from the day before.

My neighbor has an invisible dog fence. You can't see it, but if her little Jack Russell terrier dares set foot outside that fence, he gets a painful shock. All of us are like that little Jack Russell—stuck in our invisible fences.

Instead of using our thoughts to think up new ideas, to ask for the answers to life's great mysteries, we waste them on trivial, insignificant, thoroughly meaningless things. Look at the cover of a typical women's magazine:

Lose inches fast

Last-minute strategies for holiday glam

Quiz: Does your mate really love you?

Don't we have anything better to think about?

If the seven million readers of *Ladies' Home Journal* would all wonder instead, *What can I do to improve my own soul?* or *How could I make the world more loving?* the big problems we're so afraid of would be solved in a year. Seven million people concentrating on issues like that are an unstoppable force!

2. **The adman's copy.** U.S. advertisers spend more than $400 billion every year trying to convince you that without their products, you are a complete and total loser. The ad shill's entire reason for being is to make you and me dissatisfied with what we have and who we are. The average American sees between 1,500 and 3,000 commercials per day. Even non–TV watchers are constantly being invited to "consume." Everything from ATM monitors to dry-cleaning bags to stickers on supermarket fruit has been known to feature ads.

The most dangerous ads, as far as I'm concerned, are the new prescription drug ads, because they teach people to be sick. Madison Avenue has done a stellar job training us to need deodorant, mouthwash, and Domino's two-for-one pizzas. Now, they're breaking new ground by training us to be sick. Steven Pressfield, best-selling author of *The Legend of Bagger Vance* and other books, says his former ad-agency boss instructed him to "invent a disease" because "then we can sell the hell out of its cure."

3. **Other people's heads.** Like radio waves that fly around in the atmosphere, other people's thoughts constantly bombard you. You unconsciously pick up the thoughts of your family, your culture, and your religion, even if you don't actively practice it.

I once met a guy who had invented dozens of products, including many that you and I use on a daily basis. He was regularly dubbed a "genius." But if you gave him the "No Child Left Behind" test, he'd have been sent back to first grade. The guy never learned to read. And he said that was intentional.

"If I had learned to read," he said, "I'd pick up other people's ideas and cement those in my head. I choose not to bother with the interference."

This is probably the place where I should mention I'm not advocating illiteracy, just making a point that the less interference from a crazy, thought-filled world, the better your access to the FP. In fact, the reason all the spiritual *bigwigs* meditate is because it helps them avoid the interference.

4. **Your own head.** Despite what you may think you're thinking, it's quite likely there's an even bigger thought getting in the way. Unfortunately, all of us have an underlying sound track that goes something like this:

> *There's something wrong with me.*
> *I'm not good enough.*
> *I have no talent.*
> *I don't deserve it.*
> *I can't do it.*
> *It's too hard.*

Sweeping negative statements like these are what we call false prayers, the default beliefs to which you march in obedience. The good news is they're not true. The bad news is they operate *as if* they were true. They're your own personal amulet that you unwittingly carry everywhere you go. You wouldn't dream of plowing through life without them because, well, they're just so . . . familiar.

When I first began writing for magazines, I had an inferiority complex that wouldn't have fit in Shea Stadium. Because I was from a small town in the Midwest, I couldn't imagine I had anything to say to a fancy editor from New York. Although I sent query after query pitching my ideas, I didn't really expect to sell too many. After all, I just "knew" there weren't enough assignments to go around. At best, I figured I might be able to sneak a few under the radar.

Needless to say, I got a lot of rejection letters, so many that I probably could have wallpapered the city of Cincinnati, should it have needed wallpaper. The editors didn't exactly tell me to drop dead, but they didn't encourage me to keep writing, either.

Then I read a book called *Write for Your Life*, by Lawrence Block. In the early '80s, when Block's column for *Writer's Digest* was at the height of its popularity, he and his wife, Lynn, decided to throw a series of seminars for writer wannabes.

Unlike most writing seminars where you learn to write plot treatments or compose strategies to get an agent, Block's seminar dealt with the only thing that really matters when it comes to being a writer: getting out of your own way, and getting rid of the countless negative thoughts that tell you what a hopelessly uninteresting specimen of humanity you are.

At the seminar, participants meditated, grabbed partners, and confessed their greatest fears. They did all kinds of things that helped them get to the bottom of why they wanted to write, but didn't.

The seminars were hugely successful, but Block, who was a writer, not a seminar-giver, eventually got tired of trotting around the country staging events. Instead, he self-published the book I came across about the same time.

I took the book to heart. I did all of the exercises. I wrote affirmations. I consulted my inner child to find out what I was so afraid of. I even sent myself postcards for 30 days straight. On these postcards, I'd write such affirming reminders as:

- "You, Pam, are a great writer."
- "You, Pam, have what it takes to sell to New York editors."
- "You, Pam, are interesting and people want to hear what you have to say."

I'm sure the mail carrier thought I was a little cracked, wasting 25 cents (or whatever the postage was back then) to send myself postcards telling me how fascinating and abundant I was. But if he knew what a change it made in my life, he'd have been doing it, too.

Suddenly, I started getting assignments from prominent magazines—with, yes, the big New York editors. First, there was *Modern Bride,* which wanted a piece on exercises that couples could do together. *Ladies' Home Journal* asked for a travel story on Tampa Bay. Suddenly, this once-insecure writer from Kansas was getting assignments from big national magazines, the kind you see in dentists' offices.

Did I suddenly start writing more fluidly, coming up with more compelling ideas? Probably a little bit (after all, that was one of my affirmations), but mostly I changed the reality of what I thought and said about myself.

I gave up the thought there weren't enough assignments to go around. I let go of the ridiculous notion I wasn't talented enough to sell to national magazines.

Quacking in Unison

*"The main thing is to keep the main thing
the main thing."*

— T-shirt seen in Hawaii

Filmmaker Michael Moore, in a commencement speech, gave the following advice: "All you boys should learn that once you give up on that girl, she will come to you."

In some ways, our intentions work the same way. By believing we desperately need a miracle or something we don't have now, we deny Truth. We suit up with the wrong attitude.

Anytime we look for an answer, we make the false assumption that the answer isn't already here. Intending love or happiness or some other desired goal defeats the whole purpose. It assumes that the outcome of life is still in doubt. It's not.

Praying is not a matter of bribing God. It's simply understanding the higher laws that override the lower law of the physical plane. To plead or beg or to act like it's not here is to suppose duality, not unity. And unity is what we're aiming for. You have to live under the assumption that your intention has already happened. You have to feel as if it has already come to pass—to get those ducks lined up . . . to get all those waves in laser-like coherence.

I don't know if you know anything about laser technology, but it works a little bit like Congress did on September 12, 2001. Remember how all those cantankerous old senators and representatives completely forgot they were Republicans and Democrats, liberals and conservatives? How the only thing in their minds was *I'm an American, by*

God, and they sang "God Bless America" in one great, big unified chorus? Well, that's how a laser works.

Unlike ordinary light, which has lots of different types and sizes of wavelengths, lasers have wavelengths of only one size, which lends them pinpoint precision.

This is how you want to make your intentions. Or it is if you want to see something appreciable happen. Jesus didn't doubt for one second there was plenty of food to go around.

In fact, one of the reasons Jesus was crucified was that those in command thought he was altogether too confident. How dare he be so bold as to think he could make crippled people walk, lepers dance? But Jesus didn't just *think* he could do these things. He knew. He knew the truth of who he was, which made his mind a veritable laser. He didn't stop to question if a blind man could see (after all, the gift of health and perfect self-expression is everyone's divine right) or if water could become wine. He knew he had the right to command the heavens and the earth. In fact, that's the only big difference between Jesus and you and me. We're still wondering.

If you go back to Aramaic—which as you probably know, is the language in which Jesus conversed—the root word of *ask* reveals more than a "well, if it's not too much trouble." *Ask,* in Aramaic, means a combination of "claim" (as in, that deed to the land is yours) and "demand." To ask for something in prayer is to simply lay hold of what's yours. You have the right, and even the responsibility to command your life.

How can we be sure? you ask. Same way you're sure that two plus two equals four. Because it's a simple, unalterable principle of mathematics. If you add two plus two and get five, that's not the fault of mathematics. Likewise, if you're not getting the answers you want, that's not the field of potentiality's fault. It's you that's screwing up the principle. Intentions that are focused through an integrated, whole personality are like a laser—a single, clear beam.

Anecdotal Evidence

"A ship in port is safe,
but that is not what ships are built for."

— Benazir Bhutto, former prime minister of Pakistan

When he was 34, Augusten Burroughs decided to stop being an alcoholic and become a *New York Times* best-selling author. As he says in his memoir *Magical Thinking,* "The gap between active alcoholic copywriter living in squalor and literary sensation with a scrapbook of rave reviews seemed large. A virtual canyon. Yet one day, I decided that's exactly what I would do."

Fourteen days later, he finished his first manuscript, a novel called *Sellevision.*

"I did not expect it to be a bestseller. It was the cheese popcorn book. What I did expect was that it would be published," he says.

And then he wrote a memoir about his childhood.

"And this, I decided, needed to be a *New York Times* bestseller, high on the list. It needed to be translated into a dozen languages and optioned for film," he writes.

His agent suggested he tone down his ambitions.

"I understood his point of view," Augusten explains. "I also understood that the book would be huge, not because it was exceptionally well written . . . [but] because it had to be a bestseller, so I could quit my loathsome advertising job and write full time."

Augusten's memoir *Running with Scissors* spent over 70 consecutive weeks on the *New York Times* bestseller list. At last count, it has been published in over 15 countries, and was made into a film starring the incomparable Annette Bening.

"Luck? The greedy wishes of a desperate man randomly filled?" says Augusten. "No. There are no accidents."

Pray? Who, Me?

"It's bigger than the both of us, Ollie."

— Stan Laurel, English comic actor

People often tell me, "I don't pray. It's a waste of time. It's like believing in Santa Claus or the tooth fairy." My response? It's impossible to stop praying. Can't be done. Thomas Merton, the Christian mystic, said that "we pray by breathing."

Take Al Unser, for example. He didn't call it praying, but when he won his fourth Indianapolis 500 race, five days before his 48th birthday, he demonstrated the true power of prayer.

That year—1987, to be exact—he had been unceremoniously dumped from his race team even though he'd won the Indy 500 three times before. For the first time in 22 years, it looked as if he'd be forced to watch the famous race from the sidelines. His sponsors and pretty much everyone else wrote him off as "all washed up."

But in his mind, in every thought he possessed, Unser knew he was not too old to race. He knew he could still win. That "prayer" was so strong that when Danny Ongais, one of the drivers who had replaced him on the team, banged himself up in practice, Unser was brought in to race a backup car, a used March-Cosworth.

Nobody except him expected anything. Not only was he driving an older-model car, but when the familiar "Gentlemen, start your engines!" rang through the PA system, Unser was stuck back in the 20th position.

But that didn't faze the three-time winner. In every fiber of his being, he saw himself winning. He expected nothing but victory. Finally, on the 183rd lap, he worked his way up the field, crossing the line for his fourth Indianapolis 500 title. Al Unser never had a doubt. Every single thought "prayed" for victory.

Or think of the mother who, having never before picked up anything heavier than a grocery bag full of frozen foods, suddenly lifts a two-ton Plymouth off her six-year-old son, pinned underneath. At that moment, she is so thoroughly engrossed in her urgent need to free her precious child that she has no room for other thoughts. *I've got to move that car* is the only "prayer" in her mind. She does not remember, anywhere in her mind, that such an act is impossible.

The Method

"We are powerfully imprisoned by the
terms in which we have been conducted to think."

— BUCKMINSTER FULLER, AMERICAN INVENTOR AND FUTURIST

In this experiment, using nothing but the power of your thoughts, you will magnetize something into your life. You will set an intention to draw a particular event or thing into your life. Be specific down to the exact make and model.

Since you've only got 48 hours, it's probably best to pick something that won't drive your thoughts back to

"Biloxi." For example, if you decide to manifest a BMW Z3 2.8 Roadster, it's quite possible your predominant thoughts will be *Yeah right, eat my shorts.* Needless to say, thoughts like that won't take you all the way to New Orleans. Not that you couldn't manifest a BMW Z3 Roadster (there are gurus in India who pluck jewels from thin air), but, for the sake of paradigm shifting, let's start with baby steps. Pick something you can get your mind around, like a front-row theater ticket. Or flowers from your significant other.

My friend Chuck tried this experiment, and decided to be a wiseass. He wanted to sleep with two girls at one time. Sure enough, by the end of his 48 hours, he met a new woman (whom he now dates) and ended up in bed with her and her six-year-old daughter, who crawled in for a quick snuggle with her mom.

That's why it's important to be specific. And to realize that the FP has a great sense of humor.

Lab Report Sheet

The Principle: The Abracadabra Principle

The Theory: Whatever you focus on expands.

The Question: Can I pull things out of thin air simply by thinking about them?

The Hypothesis: By making the following intention and focusing on its outcome, I can draw it into my life.

My Intention: _____

_____

Time Required: 48 hours

The Approach: I have scanned over the big catalog called the world and, for the sake of this experiment, have decided that this is what I intend to manifest in the next 48 hours. I will focus on it with all my being. And I will remember what Abraham-Hicks likes to say: "It is as easy to manifest a castle as a button."

Today's Date: _____ **Time:** _____

Deadline for Manifesting: _____

Research Notes: _____

_____

:: :: ::

"A great many people think they are thinking when they are merely rearranging their prejudices."

— WILLIAM JAMES,
AMERICAN PSYCHOLOGIST AND PHILOSOPHER

EXPERIMENT #5

THE DEAR ABBY PRINCIPLE:

Your Connection to the Field Provides Accurate and Unlimited Guidance

"I have often wished that when . . . struggling with a decision or dilemma that the clouds would part, and a cosmic Charlton Heston–type voice would invite us to the second floor, where the Librarian of Life would sit with us for several hours, patiently answering all our questions and giving direction."

— HENRIETTE ANNE KLAUSER,
AUTHOR OF *WRITE IT DOWN, MAKE IT HAPPEN*

The Premise

Inner guidance is constantly available. There's never a time—never has been, never will be—when you can't get inner assistance. For anything.

Relying on any other decision-making tool is asking for trouble. The "monkey mind"—a Buddhist term for the distractible rattle, buzz-buzz, *what-should-I-do-what-do-I-do?* —was never designed to solve problems. It's like using a pair of fingernail clippers to cut the lawn. Yet, that's where most of us get our guidance—from a left cerebral hemisphere that's prone to misjudgment, faulty interpretations, and major fabrications.

The conscious mind was designed for just two things— to identify problems and formulate goals.

Anyone harnessing the mind properly would use it to define a problem or set an intention and then quickly jump back, Jack. That's it. That's all the cerebral cortex is good for. Planting seeds. But instead, the conscious mind decides to get involved, to weigh the pros and cons, to come to "rational decisions," gut feelings be damned.

No sooner does the conscious mind define the problem or set the intention than it begins the yammer, the on and on about how big the problem is and why it's not likely to get solved anytime soon and how that intention sounds cool, but . . . *Geez, I've been there, done that, and it sure as heck didn't pan out last time.* Suffice it to say, this spin doctor in the brain is not your best resource. It judges, distorts reality, and causes unnecessary emotional distress.

Let's say Jane uses her conscious mind to create the intention of improving her relationship with her husband. Perfect! Great job! Except that instead of pulling back and letting the intention flower, instead of temporarily shelving the conscious mind and turning to a source that could really offer some assistance, Jane's conscious mind begins creating "rational" conclusions, begins considering options. Before long, it's screaming, "Don't get me started."

And from there the cacophony of voices begins to sound as discordant as a band of rock-star wannabes jamming in their parents' garage:

"My relationship with my husband is a charade."

"My husband is needy and lazy."

"I'll never get what I want."

In other words, the conscious mind starts interpreting. The problem is, it can't see past its nose or past the preordained decisions it made before it was old enough to know better. The results can be messy, capricious, and cruel.

A better solution is to use those fingernail clippers for what they're designed for, put them back in the medicine cabinet, and get out a tool that's better equipped for mowing the lawn—inner guidance.

Once you get the hang of it, you'll find it's extremely reliable. Plus, its answers are far more peaceful, instinctive, and responsive to all the unpredictable factors that the conscious mind can't begin to understand.

Inner Guidance Comes in Many Packages

"I have no idea what the source of my inner voice is.
I certainly do not believe it is the voice of Jesus Christ,
or a dead ancestor with a quavery Irish brogue,
or a high-ranking Pleiadian sending me psychic
data packets from a spaceship—although that
last notion would be especially fun."

— D. Patrick Miller, founder of Fearless Books

Sometimes inner guidance comes completely unbidden. Like the night I was fretting about my newborn daughter's 106-degree temperature. I was pacing the floor with

Tasman in my arms, frantic with worry, and completely baffled as to how to bring the raging fever under control. It was around 3 A.M., and while my friends always say "Call me anytime night or day," and probably even mean it, I couldn't bring myself to do it. Instead, I walked back and forth across our little apartment. Suddenly, a voice of startling clarity surfaced in my mind. It said, *I didn't give you this great gift just to take it away.* I knew at that moment all would be well.

Sometimes inner guidance offers messages as distinct as those eight-ball fortune-telling toys. My friend Darlene had what at the time seemed like a rather foolish vision. She felt guided to apply for a music director position at her church in North Carolina. Sounded good except for one small detail: she had absolutely no musical training and could only play the alto sax—badly. Sure, she loved to sing, but loving to sing and getting a team of musicians to play instruments and singers to create harmony are two different record albums. Her conscious mind started its spin-doctoring: *Darlene, you are just plum nuts. Why would God—or anyone else—want you to lead a music team?*

So she agreed to give it one last shot—a shot from half court, no less—after which time she reassured herself she'd file the vision where it probably belonged—in the local dumpster.

She made the following bargain with her inner guidance: *If you really want me to lead the music team, have me run into either the minister, the board president, or the pianist by the end of today.* Since it was Monday and church was already sealed and delivered for that week, she figured she was safe. After all, she worked all day, and the odds of running into one of those three people in her neighborhood were next to zilch.

On the way home from work, she stopped for groceries. She walked up to the checkout line when she heard a voice: "Yoo-hoo, Darlene. What are you doing here?"

It wasn't an ethereal voice from the deep like the reassuring voice that comforted me at 3 A.M. It was the voice of Mary Jenkins, board president, who was waiting in line ahead of Darlene.

The point is that guidance comes in all packages. For many years, just before he went to sleep Napoleon Hill, author of the classic *Think and Grow Rich,* would call an imaginary council meeting of Ralph Waldo Emerson, Thomas Paine, Thomas Edison, Charles Darwin, Abraham Lincoln, Luther Burbank, Henry Ford, Napoléon, and Andrew Carnegie. As chairman of this imaginary cabinet, Hill was able to ask questions and get advice.

After some months of these nighttime proceedings, Hill was astounded that the appointees on his cabinet developed individual characteristics. Lincoln, for example, began arriving late, then walking around in solemn parade. Burbank and Paine often engaged in witty repartee.

"These experiences became so realistic that I became fearful of their consequences, and discontinued them," Hill admitted in *Think and Grow Rich.*

Like many people who receive unusual inner guidance, Hill was reluctant to admit to his nightly council meetings.

But he did say this: "While the members of my Cabinet may be purely fictional . . . they have led me into glorious paths of adventure, rekindled an appreciation of true greatness, encouraged creative endeavor, and emboldened the expression of honest thought."

Inner guidance can come in any package you're open enough to hear. Some of us need a big whack on the side of the head. Others are more like Gary Renard, author of *The*

Disappearance of the Universe, who with his extremely open mind, got guidance from a pair of ascended masters who showed up one night while he was watching TV.

Michael Beckwith, before he became a powerful New Thought minister at the Agape International Spiritual Center near Los Angeles, saw a vision of a scroll unroll that read, "Michael Beckwith to speak at the Tacoma Church of Religious Science." When the Tacoma pastor called, saying, "Hey, Michael, we'd like you to come speak at our church," Michael said, "I know."

We Put Our Inner Guidance on the No-Call List

"One of the main functions of formalized religions is to protect people against a direct experience of God."

— CARL JUNG, SWISS PSYCHIATRIST

Unfortunately, most of us have restricted the guidance we'll let in. We've decided that neon signs, telegrams, and sealed letters from God are okay, but everything else is, well, just a bit too frightening.

Hell, we'd be scared witless if a scroll unrolled in front of us or an ascended master stepped in front of the TV during an episode of *Mad Men.* Our neural pathways have said, "Uh-uh, not me, I'm not up for that." If some angel showed up at the foot of our bed, we'd probably call the police.

It has to be challenging for our inner guidance. How would you feel if someone asked you a question and then turned his or her back, ignoring everything you said?

We're like five-year-olds with our fingers in our ears going "la-la-la-la-la."

You wouldn't just pick up your phone when it rings and start talking loudly. You'd say "Hello" and listen to the person on the other end of the line. Here we are accusing the higher force of not giving us clear guidance and we're the ones with our damned phones off the hook.

When Neale Donald Walsch first sat down with a pen in his hand and some tough questions in his heart, he was shell-shocked when a voice he presumed to be God answered back, "Do you really want to know the answer? Or are you just ranting?" Walsch, who somewhat hesitantly agreed to play along, said, "Well, both. And if you've got answers, I'd love to hear them."

Where did we ever pick up the foolhardy notion that inner guidance was restricted to a lucky few? A lot of it goes back to those myths we believe about God. That he's oh-so mysterious and only on call on Sundays. The part that was left out is that our inner guidance is reliable and constantly available. It's there anytime you choose to listen, same as CNN is on anytime you decide to switch on the TV. It's that reliable.

And you are free to put it on the spot, to demand clear answers. Now.

Anecdotal Evidence

"No matter how much evidence you have, over time you tend to block out experiences that aren't 'normal.'"

— MARTHA BECK, *O* MAGAZINE COLUMNIST

Michael Beckwith, the guy I mentioned earlier who had a vision of a scroll, was looking up at a windmill one day. This is before he became a minister, when he wasn't completely convinced that his decision to pursue a Godly calling was the right one. He said point-blank, "Look, God, if you're listening, if this is what you really want for me, have that windmill point in my direction."

Even though it was a windy day and the windmill was spinning very fast in the other direction, no sooner did he say that than the windmill stopped rotating on its normal axis and pointed straight at him.

Of course, he'd already had one or two mind-blowing experiences. To put himself through school (this is back when he wanted to be a doctor), Beckwith sold drugs—just to his friends, of course. Since he was a gregarious, open kind of guy, let's just say his business flourished. His marijuana dealership grew to both coasts, and convinced him that if he played his cards right, he could retire completely by the age of 24.

But he knew something was off. His inner guidance kept prodding, giving him bizarre dreams, strongly suggesting there had to be a better way. He decided on his own to give up drugs, to follow that "better way." He told all his friends that it was over: he was retiring. On his final drug deal (the one that would get rid of the last of his supplies), he was busted by federal agents. Now, keep in mind that not only did he have in his possession 100 pounds of pot, but he also had large sums of cash, guns, and hot cameras.

Still, his inner voice told him, "Everything is going to be okay."

As he prepared for trial, his friends thought he was crazy. "Why aren't you fretting, pacing the floor, thinking up strategies for getting out of this bad rap?" they asked him.

"I was guilty," he says. "But I was also assured by God that everything was going to be okay."

By that time, he'd seen a grander vision. He went to trial (his attorney was Robert Shapiro, pre-O.J. days, then just launching his career), peaceful and believing that no matter what, he was loved and cared for by this very real presence. Sure enough, he got off on a technicality, and when the judge freed him with the comment that he never wanted to see him again, Michael knew that he never would.

Sometimes, the field of infinite possibilities even manages to get through to people who scoff at it. In 1975 Gerald Jampolsky, at the time a successful California psychiatrist on the "outside," was falling apart on the inside. His 20-year marriage had ended. He was drinking heavily. He developed chronic, disabling back pain. Of course, it never dawned on him to seek higher guidance.

As he says, "I was the last person to be interested in a thought system that used words like *God* and *love*."

But nonetheless, when he first saw *A Course in Miracles*, the book I've mentioned a few times that teaches personal transformation by choosing love rather than fear, he heard a voice clearly tell him, "Physician, heal thyself. This is your way home."

And of course, it was. Jampolsky has gone on to write many books. He lectures widely on the principles of *A Course in Miracles*, and he even started a center in Sausalito, California, for people with life-threatening illnesses.

Immediate, direct guidance is available 24/7. But instead of paying attention, we taught ourselves the most unnatural habit of not listening. It's like the foreign-exchange student who didn't grow up around technology and has no idea that the phone beside his bed could hook him up with that cute girl in his biology class. He thinks he has to wait until tomorrow to talk to her. It's like that overlooked space heater I mentioned in the Preface.

More Anecdotal Evidence

"If only God would give me a clear sign. Like making a large deposit in my name at a Swiss bank."

— WOODY ALLEN,
AMERICAN FILMMAKER

When she was 25, actress Jamie Lee Curtis was hanging out in her recently purchased Los Angeles apartment with her friend Debra Hill. Debra, who had produced *Halloween,* the spooky movie that launched Curtis's career, had brought over the current issue of *Rolling Stone* magazine as a housewarming gift. They were flipping through the magazine and chatting optimistically about the end of Jamie Lee's most recent relationship when they saw a photograph of three men.

Jamie Lee pointed to the man on the right, who was wearing a plaid shirt and a waggish smirk, and told Debra, "I'm going to marry that man."

She'd never seen him before and had no idea who he was, but something inside told her he was "the one."

"That's Christopher Guest," Debra said. "He's in a funny new movie called *This Is Spinal Tap.* I know his agent."

Jamie Lee, awestruck by this very clear churning in her gut, called the agent the next day, gave him her number, and told him to have Chris call her if he was interested.

He never called.

Several months later, while at Hugo's, a popular West Hollywood restaurant, Jamie Lee glanced up to find herself staring straight at the guy from the magazine, who was only three tables away. He waved as if to say, "I'm the guy you called." She waved back.

Hmm, she thought. *Interesting.* Except a few minutes later, he got up to leave. He shrugged, waved, and walked out the door. Jamie Lee looked down at her plate, kicking herself for believing in something as stupid as "inner guidance."

But the next day, her phone rang. It was Chris Guest and he wanted to set up a date. Four days later, at Chianti Ristorante on Melrose, they met for dinner. By the time Guest left for New York to tape an episode of *Saturday Night Live* just over one month later, they'd fallen deeply, passionately in love.

Soon after, when they were talking on the phone, Chris said to Jamie, "I was out walking along Fifth Avenue today."

"Oh yeah," Jamie said. "What'd you do there?"

"Ah, do you like diamonds?" he asked.

They were married on December 18, 1984, eight months after Jamie Lee Curtis got that initial guidance.

The Method

> *"Parting the Red Sea, and turning water to blood, the burning bush . . . nothing like that was going on now. Not even in New York City."*
>
> — MICHAEL CRICHTON, AUTHOR OF *JURASSIC PARK*

In this experiment, we'll prove that the guidance received by Jamie Lee Curtis and others is not some weird, *Twilight Zone*–like anomaly, but a very real and ongoing tool that all of us can use at any time.

You'll spend 48 hours expecting a specific, concrete answer to a specific, concrete question. It can be as simple as whether to adopt a new Siamese kitten or as complicated as whether or not to take a job offer. Either way, give your inner guidance 48 hours to spell it out. But watch out. I tried this once and got fired. In retrospect, however, it was the perfect answer, maybe the only one I could hear to the question I'd asked: "Is it time to launch my freelance writing career?"

Choose an issue that is troubling you, something that has a yes or no answer, something on which you're really confused and don't know what to do. I know you're thinking of something right now, doesn't matter what it is. That issue will work. Look at your watch.

Ask for a clear, non-debatable answer and ask for it to show up within the next 48 hours. It might show up immediately. It might take only a day, but within 48 hours, expect to have a neon sign of an answer.

It's your job to set the intention and the time frame. The FP will do the rest.

Stan (remember the cute former surfer from Esalen I mentioned in the Preface?) had lost his job. To make matters worse, his girlfriend of three years decided it was time to move on. Needless to say, he had some pretty serious decisions to make. First on the agenda, Stan decided, was to find a way to make some money. But he had no idea what he wanted to do. I reminded him there was a divine plan for his life and that it would be revealed if he simply set the intention and a clear deadline.

Stan said something like this: "Hey, dude, if it's true you have a plan for my life, I could use a directional pointer. I don't have a lot of time, so by Friday morning, I want to know just what you have in mind for me."

On Thursday afternoon, Stan was sitting in the hot springs with a man he'd never met. The man happened to mention he was opening a self-improvement center out in Pennsylvania's Laurel Highlands and was looking for someone to run the place. Stan immediately felt a buzz and, sure enough, less than 30 minutes later, he was offered the job, even though the sum total of his job experience at a self-improvement center was that of cabin cleaner.

Chalk one up for the FP!

Lab Report Sheet

The Principle: The Dear Abby Principle

The Theory: Your connection to the field provides accurate and unlimited guidance.

The Question: Is it really possible to get ongoing, immediate guidance?

The Hypothesis: If I ask for guidance, I will get a clear answer to the following yes-or-no question: _____

_____

Time Required: 48 hours

Today's Date: _____ **Time:** _____

Deadline for Receiving Answer: _____

The Approach: All right, here goes: "Okay, inner guidance, I need to know the answer to this question. You've got 48 hours. Make it snappy."

Research Notes: _____

_____

⸭ ⸭ ⸭

"Man, surrounded by facts, permitting himself no surprise, no intuitive flash, no great hypothesis, no risk, is in a locked cell. Ignorance cannot seal the mind more securely."

— ALBERT EINSTEIN, GERMAN THEORETICAL PHYSICIST

EXPERIMENT #6

THE SUPERHERO PRINCIPLE:

Your Thoughts and Consciousness Impact Matter

"The course of the world is not predetermined by physical laws . . . the mind has the power to affect groups of atoms and even tamper with the odds of atomic behavior."

— SIR ARTHUR STANLEY EDDINGTON,
ENGLISH MATHEMATICIAN AND ASTROPHYSICIST

The Premise

Japanese scientist Dr. Masaru Emoto spent 15 years researching the effects of human speech, thoughts, and emotions on physical matter. Dr. Emoto chose one of matter's four traditional elements—water—to see how it responds to words, music, prayers, and blessings. Using more than 10,000 samples of water, Emoto and his research assistants spoke to, played music for, and asked monks to recite prayers over the water. The samples were then frozen, and the resulting ice crystals were examined under a microscope.

In case you're wondering what water has to do with anything, dig this: Water is present everywhere—even in the air—and since the human body and, indeed, the earth consist of 70 percent water, it stands to reason that if words and thoughts impact water on its own, they will also affect larger, more complex systems also made up of water.

What Emoto found is that when scientists treated the water "kindly," by saying such things as "I love you" and "thank you," the resulting water crystals became clear and beautifully formed. But when Emoto and his team talked negatively to the water, screaming such snide comments as "I hate you!" or "You idiot!" the crystals formed dark, ugly holes. When Elvis Presley's "Heartbreak Hotel" was played, the resulting frozen crystal split in two.

In one photo, he shows how a sample from the dam at Fujiwara Lake, starting out as a dark and amorphous blob, is completely transformed after a priest prays over it for just one hour. The ugly crystal turned into a clear, bright-white hexagonal crystal-within-a-crystal. He also found that prayer could create new types of crystals that had never before been seen.

We in the West are not taught about energy and the power of our body/mind. Instead of being trained to tune in to our innate intelligence, we're told, "Here's a doctor. Here's a nurse. When something's wrong, consult with them." Coaches tell us if we're good enough to make the basketball team. Teachers tell us if our art is up to snuff. We're taught to turn over our power to forces outside ourselves.

The Power of Perception

*"My mind is a bad neighborhood
I try not to go into alone."*

— ANNE LAMOTT, AMERICAN AUTHOR

When I was born on February 17, 1956, my father took one look at me, lying there helplessly in my pink basinet, and announced to my mother that I was the ugliest baby he had ever seen. Needless to say, my mother was devastated. And for me, a minutes-old human being, it was decided that beauty—or lack thereof—was destined to color every moment of my life.

My dad's life-changing indictment was prompted by my nose, which was plastered to my face like a roadkill possum. After my mother was in labor for 18 grueling hours, her obstetrician decided to intervene with a pair of cold metal forceps. In the battle between the forceps and me, my nose got flattened.

Gradually, the nose bounced back to normal, but my fragile ego remained disfigured. I desperately wanted to be beautiful. I wanted to prove to my father that I was acceptable and to make up to my mother for the embarrassment I caused her.

I scoured beauty magazines, studying the models like a biologist studies cells. I rolled my hair with orange-juice cans and ordered green face masks and blackhead pumps from the back of *Seventeen* magazine. I saved my allowance to buy a set of Clairol electric rollers. I wore gloves to bed to keep the hand-softening Vaseline from staining the sheets. I even clipped "interesting" hairstyles from the Montgomery Ward catalog, pasting them to the back page of my own personal "beauty book."

This personal beauty book, besides the 50 heads with different hairstyles, listed my beauty goals: reduce my waist by five inches, increase my bust size by six inches, grow my hair, and so on. I even included a page with plans for accomplishing each goal. To reduce my waist, for example, I would do 50 sit-ups each day, limit my morning pancake consumption to two, and give up Milky Way bars.

Despite my well-meaning attempts, I remained less than beautiful. No matter what I did, I never could seem to get my looks together. How could I? My very existence centered around my dad's ugly-baby statement. It was the first sentence about my life, the proclamation around which my very life revolved. To go against it would dishonor everything I knew—my dad, my mom, myself.

Things went from bad to worse. By sixth grade, my eyesight weakened and I was forced to wear a pair of black horn-rimmed glasses. By ninth grade, when I finally convinced Dad to invest in contact lenses, a definite beauty booster, my face immediately broke out in a connect-the-dots puzzle of pimples. All my babysitting money went for Clearasil, astringent, and Angel Face Makeup. One summer, after I heard zits were caused by chocolates and soft drinks, I even gave up Coca-Cola and candy bars.

And if that wasn't bad enough, my sister, who had the good fortune to escape both the forceps and the ugliness indictment, pointed out that my front teeth were crooked. Once again, I campaigned for family funds to install braces.

The sad thing about all this work and effort is that it was futile. I had no idea that until I changed the deep-seated thoughts about myself, I'd remain "ugly." I could have exercised, applied makeup, and rolled my hair unto eternity, but as long as my dad's indictment was the thought virus on which I operated, I was destined to be the "ugliest baby" he'd ever seen. Oh, sure, I made temporary progress. I'd clear up my complexion or grow my hair or straighten my teeth, but before long, something else would happen to resume the old familiar "ugliness."

You see, my body had no choice but to follow the blueprints my thoughts had given it.

About this time, I discovered self-help books. It was an inevitable meeting. Any college freshman who thinks she closely resembles Frankenstein needs all the self-esteem boosting she can find.

I started with *Your Erroneous Zones,* by Dr. Wayne Dyer. I read Barbara Walters's book on how to make conversation. I learned how to win friends and influence people, how to empower myself with positive thinking, and how to think and grow rich. All the reading eventually started to change the way I felt about myself. I actually started finding things I liked.

Even things about my looks. I was tall, for one thing, which meant I could more or less eat anything I wanted and not gain weight. And my thick hair was an asset. And my best friend's mother said I had perfectly shaped eyebrows. Instead of looking for things I disliked, I started concentrating on things I *liked.* Like magic, my looks started improving. As I gave up the limiting thoughts, I began to see my own beauty. The less I chastised that poor little ogre in the mirror, the more she started to change. The less I *tried* to change myself, the more I changed.

Miraculously, my eyesight returned to normal. I was finally able to throw away the Coke-bottle glasses and the contacts. The complexion from hell cleared up, and my teeth, after months of using a retainer, began to match the even teeth of the other members of my family. In fact, the only time I felt grotesquely ugly was when I'd visit my dad and his second wife.

Although I didn't realize it at the time, I was changing my "looks" during those visits to satisfy my dad's belief about me—or rather what I thought were his beliefs about me. I now know my dad's remark was simply an offhand comment. He meant no harm.

But because I didn't know it at the time, I took his ugly-baby comment to heart and acted it out in rich, vivid detail.

Even the poor eyesight, which some might argue is a genetic propensity, was solely my creation. Nobody else in my family (there were five of us) ever wore glasses. Everyone else had 20/20 vision. Likewise, nobody else in my family wore braces. They all had picture-perfect teeth.

Anecdotal Evidence

"Henceforth I whimper no more, postpone no more, need nothing. From this hour, I ordain myself loos'd of limits and imaginary lines."

— WALT WHITMAN, AMERICAN POET

Sickness is optional. I should probably have my head examined for including this section in the book. You'll notice I've hidden it in the middle of a long chapter near the back.

It's not that you haven't heard ideas like this before—that so-and-so's cancer was caused by unresolved anger or that stress can turn hair white overnight. But what I'm going so far as to say is that we've been led down the garden path by a bloated, greedy medical system that has convinced us that disease is inevitable. I am not knocking doctors, nurses, or other medical personnel, 99.9 percent of whom are caring, committed, and well-meaning. No, they're just as hoodwinked as we are.

What I'm suggesting is that the erroneous conscious-ness of all of us has resulted in major "computer glitches." Instead of seeing sickness as a problem, something to cor-rect, we accept it as a fact of life. We've all agreed to this arbitrary set of rules that says sickness can't be escaped, illness is natural. Most of us can't even imagine perfect health.

Long ago, our minds established this false pattern of perception. Once a mind thinks it can't do some task (like unclog an artery), it informs the brain that it can't do it, which in turn informs the muscles. The "virus" in our con-sciousness has limited our ability to utilize our bodies' great wisdom.

But our belief in the inevitability of a degenerating body only seems real because we've believed it to be real for so long. Dr. Alexis Carrel, a French physician and Nobel Prize winner, demonstrated that cells can be kept alive indefi-nitely. His research proved "there's no reason cells need to degenerate. Ever."

"The education we all get is that we have no power, that we don't know anything," explains Meir Schneider, a man who cured himself of blindness, "but it's not true. Within each of us is everything we need to know."

When he was born in Lviv, Ukraine, in 1954, Schneider was cross-eyed and had glaucoma, astigmatism, nystag-mus, and several other hard-to-pronounce diseases that affect the eyes. His cataracts were so severe that he was forced to endure five major surgeries before he turned seven. The last one broke the lens on his eyeball, and by the time he was in second grade, he was declared legally blind. So much for modern medicine.

When Schneider was 17, he met a kid named Isaac with a different message than that of the doctors and surgeons. Isaac, who was a year younger than he was, actually had the gall to tell him, "If you want, you can train yourself to see."

No one had ever had that kind of faith before. All Schneider had ever heard before this was, "you poor, poor blind thing."

Meir Schneider's family, like any good, sympathetic family, discouraged him from getting his hopes up. "Sure, try the exercises," they said, "but don't forget—you're a blind kid." Within a year, as Isaac predicted, Meir began to see—not a lot at first, but enough to believe that maybe this 16-year-old kid knew more than the doctors who wrote him off as blind and inoperable.

Eventually Schneider gained enough vision to read, walk, run, and even drive. Today, he proudly possesses a California driver's license, and he operates a self-healing center.

"Blind people," he says, "become more blind because they aren't expected to see. They're thrown into a category."

Furthermore, he can't understand why an optimistic concept sounds so bizarre to most people.

When Barbra Streisand was a young girl growing up in Brooklyn, she fell in love with the movies. She wanted nothing more than to be a glamorous movie star. Unfortunately, her widowed mother was dirt-poor, and Barbra wasn't exactly Grace Kelly material. Any reasonable career counselor would have encouraged her to pursue a different goal. "After all, honey, you have an unconventional nose and . . . well, how can I put this politely? You being an actress is like Kareem Abdul-Jabbar wanting to be a jockey."

But Barbra's intentions were *so* strong that I believe she manipulated circumstances through the only pathway she could—by manifesting a voice so powerful that it led to stardom on Broadway and eventually to the movies.

Roll your eyes and call me deluded, but here are the facts: no one else in Barbra's family could sing. No one else had any musical talent.

Matter Does Not Control You— You Control Matter

"We would rather be ruined than changed.
We would rather die in our dread than climb
the cross of the moment and let our illusions die."

— W. H. Auden, Anglo-American poet

When Terry McBride was 22, he ruptured a disk in his back while working construction. After a year of visiting a chiropractor and trying osteopathy and muscle relaxers, he decided to take the suggestion of an orthopedic surgeon who thought he should have his spine fused.

"I was told I'd be in the hospital for a couple weeks, home for a couple of weeks, in a brace for six months, and then as good as new," McBride explained at a talk I once heard him give.

Two days after the surgery, he came down with a dangerously high fever. He was rushed back to the hospital where doctors discovered that somehow during the surgery he had contracted the *E. coli* bacteria. During the next year, he had eight surgical procedures to try to get rid of the spreading infection. By the fifth surgery, he was transferred to the teaching hospital at University of Washington, where, as he notes, "I was a celebrity. I had the worst case of osteomyelitis they'd ever seen."

On the night before yet another surgery, his team of doctors walked somberly into his room. They'd finally gotten accurate x-rays, which showed the infection was no longer just in his spine. It had spread to his pelvis and abdomen, and down both legs. To get rid of it, they said, they were going to have to cut him open from end to end. They said that by doing this procedure, they could virtually guarantee they'd get rid of the infection. But they could also guarantee that he'd lose the use of his right leg.

"Now, I'd studied under one of the great metaphysicians—John Wayne—and when someone in the movies told the Duke they had to remove his leg, he said, 'That's okay, do it anyway,'" McBride points out. But then the doctor went on to say that if the infection were as bad as they all thought, he could also lose his *left* foot and control of his bowels and bladder, and there was a good chance he'd end up sexually impotent.

"Quite honestly," McBride says, "that's where they made their mistake.

"Now I don't know about you, but I showed up on this planet as a happy little boy who liked myself. But it didn't take long to learn that the people in authority knew more about me than I did. I learned that I needed to pay attention and that it was the teachers who were going to tell me how good I was in school. The coaches were gonna decide if I had any athletic ability. I learned early on to look outside myself for who I was.

"Now, I probably would have given them a leg," McBride continues. "But when those doctors started insisting that there was no possible way to come out of this surgery whole, I decided right then and there that nobody was going to tell me who I was. I decided that very night that no longer was anyone with a fancy name badge going to determine my destiny."

It was the night that changed his life. McBride, who had been studying spiritual principles, announced to the whole room (the team of five doctors, his wife, and his two-year-old daughter) that there was a power in the universe and he was going to use it to make him whole and free.

When he had first started saying such things, everybody had remarked, "Right on! Hold fast to your dreams." But after ten surgeries, people began urging him to "face reality," to quit focusing on his petty, ego-centered personal priorities.

"We're talking petty, ego-centered personal priorities such as having a body that was disease free, a back that was strong enough to pick up my daughter, petty, ego-centered priorities like going to the bathroom without a plastic bag," he says. "Some people started suggesting that maybe perfect health wasn't part of God's plan."

"Even as a good fundamentalist, I couldn't buy that I deserved eighteen surgeries. Maybe I'd sinned enough for four or five, but not eighteen," McBride explains.

He was sent to talk to the hospital psychiatrist who sat him down and said, "Son, it's time to take off the rose-colored glasses. Now you think that to be a man, you've got to be able to stand on two legs, to fight in the war like your father did, but it's time to come work with me, to learn to accept that you're going to spend the rest of your life in a wheelchair."

He showed him his medical records, which clearly stated: "Terry McBride's problems are not curable. He will have permanent disability and ongoing surgeries for the rest of his life."

"But I'm not my medical records," McBride insisted. "I'm not my past. There is a power in me. I live in a spiritual universe and spiritual law can set me free."

"Don't you think your body would have healed by now if it was going to be healed?" the psychiatrist asked.

But McBride refused to give up. He went on to have 30 major surgeries over the course of 11 years, and wore a colostomy bag. All the while he continued to affirm that health and wholeness was his spiritual destiny.

Finally, long after most of us would have given up, he walked out of the hospital a free and whole strapping young man. Today, he travels the country speaking about his journey, teaching people the truth about their divine magnificence.

As he says, "We are already free. The infinite power of God will back up our belief in sickness and want if that's what we choose. But we can also change our beliefs to health, love, joy, and peace. It's time to claim our oneness with God, to step boldly into our lives. You are God and this is the truth that will set you free."

The Method

> *"There are no limitations to the self*
> *except those you believe in."*

— Seth, disembodied teacher channeled by Jane Roberts

Since we don't have access to all of Masaru Emoto's microscopes and research assistants, we're going to affect matter by duplicating an experiment you might have tried back in grade school—namely, sprouting green-bean seeds. Dr. Larry Dossey, in more than a half dozen books on prayer, has detailed fastidiously precise medical studies that have proven that intention on a particular physical outcome affects everything from rye seeds to women with breast cancer. Again, we're beginners, so we're going to start with green beans.

Equipment:

- ⊞ Cardboard egg carton
- ⊞ Potting soil
- ⊞ Green-bean seeds

Instructions: Plant two beans in each of the 12 slots of the egg carton, and place it near a window. Water the plants every couple of days. Make the following conscious intention: *With my innate energy, I will that the beans on the left side of the egg carton grow faster than the beans on the right.*

Write down your observations for the next seven days. *Voilà*—by the end of the week, you should see evidence that your intention has manifested.

In the meantime, you can experiment with something scientists call *applied kinesiology.* It may sound complicated, but it's really just an elementary method of testing how your body reacts to negative and positive statements, spoken aloud. Dr. John Goodheart pioneered applied kinesiology in the '60s when he discovered that muscles instantly became weak when the body was exposed to harmful substances, and strong in the presence of anything therapeutic. In the next decade, Dr. John Diamond discovered that muscles also respond to emotional and intellectual stimuli.

Touch the thumb and middle finger of each hand to form two rings. Now link them together. Pull the linked fingers of the right hand tightly against the left hand, exerting just enough pressure so they hold. Get a feel for how that feels.

Now say your name aloud: "My name is _____." At the same time, exert the same amount of pressure. Since I'm assuming you're not telling a fib, this statement will probably show that your hand stays strong and steady.

Now say: "My name is Julia Roberts." Even if you exert the same amount of pressure as before, the fingers should break apart.

Try several true and false statements until you get the calibration down. If the circle holds, it indicates a positive response; if the fingers of the right hand were able to break the connection of your left hand, the answer is "no way."

Not only is this an effective tool for getting your body's advice, but it's also useful for testing how your body responds to differing statements such as the following:

- "I am a huge dorkball."
- "I am loving, passionate, peaceful, and happy."
- "I hate my body."
- "I am strong and powerful."

Lab Report Sheet

The Principle: The Superhero Principle

The Theory: Your thoughts and consciousness impact matter.

The Question: Is it possible to affect the physical world with my attention?

The Hypothesis: If I focus my attention on a row of green-bean seeds, I can make them sprout faster.

Time Required: Seven days

Today's Date: _____ **Time:** _____

The Approach: I will focus my attention on a row of green beans. I will send those seeds positive vibes and expect them to be influenced by my energy.

Research Notes: _____

_____

∷ ∷ ∷

"People need to realize that their thoughts are more primary than their genes, because the environment, which is influenced by our thoughts, controls the genes."
— BRUCE LIPTON, PH.D., AMERICAN CELL BIOLOGIST

EXPERIMENT #7

THE JENNY CRAIG PRINCIPLE:

Your Thoughts and Consciousness Provide the Scaffolding for Your Physical Body

"Your body is simply a living expression of your point of view about the world."

— CARL FREDERICK,
AUTHOR OF *EST PLAYING THE GAME: THE NEW WAY*

The Premise

The environment in which you live responds to your thoughts and emotions. To prove this in a very observable fashion, you're going to use your bathroom scale. Yes, this is the experiment where you offer your body up to science. But don't worry. It's just for three days. And the end result is something 90 percent of us, at least according to a study at Cornell University, are actively trying to do anyway: lose weight. For those two or three lucky devils who are hoping to *gain* weight, well, you can expect an increase in your health and vitality.

Your food, like everything else in the world, is infused with energy, and by working with it instead of fighting against it (as most of us do in our obsession to lose weight), you'll easily drop a pound or two without changing a single thing.

The specific premise for this experiment is that the energy provided by your food is affected by what you say and think. Those items on your dinner plate are not static lumps of nutrition, but rather morsels of dynamic energy that eavesdrop on every one of your intentions. And while nutritionists can't exactly quantify your thoughts to include them on food labels, they probably should if they want to make an accurate assessment of what that can of pork and beans or that package of pasta means to your health. The energy of your thoughts is being ingested right along with the calcium and vitamin D.

If you haven't already seen it, rent the documentary film *I Am* by Tom Shadyac. The whole movie is amazing, but for the research purposes of this experiment, pay careful attention to the scene where Shadyac, a famous Hollywood director, visits the Institute of HeartMath, a non-profit research organization that studies stress and human energy. First, Rollin McCraty, the institute's longtime director of research, hooks electrodes to a bowl of yogurt.

Although yogurt is widely regarded as an inert blob, McCraty uses the electrodes to demonstrate that it responds to Shadyac's thoughts and emotions. The needle on the bioresponse meter oscillated wildly when he was asked about an earlier marriage. It flew off the charts when he mentioned his lawyer, with whom he confirmed he had unfinished business. The yogurt, without being attached to Shadyac in any way, was able to read his emotions. When he brought his attention back to the present, back to the room, the needle went still.

"We don't exactly know how this works, but we have irrefutable proof that human emotions create a very real energetic field to which other living systems are attuned," McCraty says.

So think about it. How many times have you said or thought something like the following?

- *It's really hard for me to lose weight.*
- *I just look at a piece of chocolate cake and gain weight.*
- *I have a slow metabolism.*

Not only do thoughts like this make you feel like warmed-over dog doo, but they radically affect your body and what you put into it.

In the 1960s, Cleve Backster, a former CIA agent, made headlines when he discovered that plants perceive human intentions. In 1966, after retiring from the CIA, Backster started what is still considered to be the world's largest lie-detection agency. One night, while sitting in his New York office, he decided to attach a galvanometer to a houseplant. It was a fluke, just something to kill time. What he discovered was that the dracaena that his secretary had brought in to decorate the office reacted not just to physical harm (he dunked its leaves in hot coffee and burned them with a match), but to his very thoughts and intentions. He was shocked and felt like "running into the street and shouting to the world, 'Plants can think!'" Instead, he plunged into a meticulous investigation to establish just how the plant was reacting to his thoughts.

Using highly sophisticated polygraph equipment, he was able to prove that plants—all kinds of plants—react to human thoughts and emotions. He tested dozens of different varieties, ones we humans eat on a daily basis. He discovered that plants respond to sounds that are inaudible to the human ear and to wavelengths of infrared and ultraviolet light, which are invisible to the human eye.

Viennese biologist Raoul Francé, who died in 1943, before such intricate instrumentation was available, had already suggested that plants constantly observe and record events and phenomena of which humans—trapped in our anthropocentric view of the world—know nothing.

So why is this relevant to our bathroom scales? Of the average ton of food we consume each year, the bulk comes from plants. Granted, it's often processed and beat and spun so as to be almost unrecognizable, but much of our food starts as living, sentient plants. The remainder of our food comes from animals, which—guess what?—also get their energy from plants. So nearly all the food, drink, intoxicants, and medicines that keep us alive are derived from plants, which Backster and many scientists who followed have proved are able to read your thoughts.

Are you getting what I'm saying?

What you think and say about yourself, your body, and your food is the hinge upon which your health turns. Counting calories and fat grams with religious zealotry may well be the main obstacle between you and your ideal weight.

Food Fight

"The more obsessed one is with getting thin,
the more certain it becomes that one
will never get there."

— AUGUSTEN BURROUGHS, AMERICAN AUTHOR

Diets are the enemy. They make you paranoid, insane, and fat. It doesn't take a rocket scientist to figure out that diets don't work. So why do we persist in depriving and disciplining ourselves in the name of diets when they obviously suck sewer slime. Think of it like this: If you went to collect your paycheck and your boss said, "Sorry, but we've decided not to pay you this week," would you keep working at that job, week after week, hoping that someday he'd have a change of heart? Even the spelling of the word should give us a clue. Who wants to do anything with the word *die* in it?

Suffice it to say, most of us have a very complex relationship with food. Just ask the $60-billion-a-year diet industry. Instead of enjoying food's awesome and life-giving nourishment, we fear it, despise it, and blame it for the picture we see in the mirror. Can anyone say *love-hate relationship?*

As long as you harbor negative energy about yourself and spend time *wanting* to lose weight, that's what you'll get: negativity and "the state of wanting to lose weight."

Not only is this type of thinking counterproductive, but it keeps you stuck with the body you're currently in. Your body is a barometer of your belief system. Your cells eavesdrop on everything you say and think, and by making disparaging comments about your jiggly forearms or turning over the same thought again and again about the inner tube around your waist, you're stamping them into the muscles, glands, and tissues of your body.

This may come as a shock to you—especially if you spend most of your waking moments silently harping about your ugly, cellulite-ridden body—but the normal state of your body is healthy. It can heal and regulates itself without any prompting from you. But when you keep tabs and count calories with frenetic abandon, you refuse to let your body change.

Anecdotal Evidence

"Our body is a walking crystal. We store electro-magnetic energy. We can receive, we can transmit and we can store electro-magnetic energy."

— DR. C. NORMAN SHEALY,
AMERICAN HOLISTIC RESEARCH PHYSICIAN AND NEUROSURGEON

When Alan Finger, a now-famous yoga teacher, was in his teens, he lost 100 pounds in—are you sitting down?—one month.

After studying in India, his father, Mani Finger, brought back a powerful yogic breathing program that he taught to his overweight son.

Within one month of using the breathing exercises, a powerful tool for moving energy, Alan dropped 100 pounds.

I know what you're thinking. That's impossible, it can't be done.

So let me stop you right there. Thoughts like that, thoughts that scoff at infinite possibility, are getting in your way. To change your energy you have to change your thinking. The word *impossible* should not be part of your vocabulary.

A friend of mine had been trying to lose weight for probably 30 years. She tried everything, including exercise and consuming tiny amounts of food. Nothing worked. She finally consulted with an Emotional Freedom Technique (EFT) specialist even though she had trouble believing that something as simple as tapping on the body's meridian points could actually be effective at winning the weight battle she'd fought for so many years. But she was desperate. Within a month of unblocking her stuck energy, she lost every one of those stubborn pounds. She has been able to keep off that weight, and still looks fabulous today.

As for Alan Finger losing 100 pounds in one measly month (you can read about it in *Breathing Space,* a book he wrote with fellow yoga teacher Katrina Repka), what do you have to lose by believing it's possible?

I also highly recommend a book called *The Biology of Belief,* by Bruce Lipton. He's a cell biologist who used to teach at Stanford University. He discovered that, despite what we all believe, our bodies are influenced more by energy and the thoughts we have than they are by our DNA.

Lipton tells a remarkable story about a group of patients with problematic knees. The first group underwent complicated knee surgery. The second group believed that they, too, had had the surgery. But the doctor conducting the research made the incisions on the second group, but didn't actually operate. So nothing about their knees was changed. Both groups, however, got better. Both groups were soon able to walk and play basketball and do all the things they had done before their knee injuries.

Now, that's a pretty strong placebo effect and should be proof positive that you need to see yourself as thin and gorgeous, negative thinking be damned. Whatever you focus on in your life expands, as Experiment #5 demonstrates. So if you focus on being fat and needing to diet, that "reality" is going to expand in your life.

The Method

> *"Life itself is the proper binge."*
>
> — JULIA CHILD, AMERICAN AUTHOR, CHEF, AND TV PERSONALITY

In this experiment, you're going to give up your ongoing grudge against the food you eat. You're going to think of every single morsel that enters your body as your best friend, or at least a thoroughly nourishing acquaintance.

Energy worker Thomas Hanna says that when we look at a person's body, we're observing the moving process of that person's mind. It's our beliefs about ourselves, more than the banana-cream pie we couldn't resist, that cause us to gain weight.

So for starters in this experiment, you're going to refrain from saying anything negative about your body. You may notice this is hard to do. Every time you make a disparaging comment, turn it around—if not out loud, then at least silently to yourself. For example, your best friend calls and without thinking you blurt out, "I ate a whole bag of buttered popcorn at the movie yesterday. I probably gained eight pounds." Cancel it by saying something like, "Well, I did spill half the bag when Antonio Banderas took off his shirt, and I actually think I look thinner." (You don't have to be modest. It's okay to admit that you're a knockout!)

Food is full of energetic juju, and eating should be a thoroughly positive experience. We've gotten so far off track on this that this experiment could be the very hardest for most people to undertake.

Because feeling guilt about food is such an ingrained habit, this might feel completely unnatural. It might take some practice. You might even have to repeat this experiment if you notice the old patterns creeping back in, if you find yourself wondering how many calories or fat grams you're about to consume. That's why this experiment takes 72 hours rather than the 48 hours of most of the other experiments.

What we're looking to prove is that your thoughts and energy are in a continual dance with the world around you.

Remember when people used to pray before meals? My family always did, even at restaurants, which embarrassed me to no end when I was in junior high. Now I know those prayers put positive energy and good thoughts into the food—not that we were conscious of it at the time. But I must tell you that nobody in my family has ever had much of a weight problem.

So during this experiment, you're going to do the following:

1. Refrain from talking "smack" about your body. If possible, refrain from negativity of any kind.

2. Before you put anything into your body, send it loving thoughts, put your hands over it, and give it a blessing.

3. Concentrate on infusing your food with love, joy, and peace.

That's it. Weigh yourself the day you start, and again three days later.

■■ ■■ ■■

Lab Report Sheet

The Principle: The Jenny Craig Principle

The Theory: Your thoughts and consciousness provide the scaffolding for your physical body.

The Question: Does what I think affect my environment—specifically, the food I take into my body?

The Hypothesis: If my thoughts and consciousness are in a continuous dance with my environment, the food I eat can't help but be affected by my thoughts. By changing what I think about and say to my food, I will be healthier and, for the sake of this experiment, lose at least one pound.

Time Required: 72 hours

Today's Date: _____

Weight as Recorded First Thing in the Morning: _____

Weight as Recorded First Thing in the Morning, Three Days Later: _____

The Approach: Don't change a single thing about your diet. In fact, what you eat should be a nonissue during the time period of this experiment. However, every time you do eat something over the next three days, whether it's your morning over-easy eggs or an afternoon slice of a co-worker's birthday cake, deliberately and consciously send the food positive, loving thoughts before ingesting it. Thank it for nourishing you and expect it to contribute to the betterment of your body.

Research Notes: _____

_____

⠿ ⠿ ⠿

"You manufacture beauty with your mind."

— Augusten Burroughs, American author

EXPERIMENT #8

THE 101 DALMATIANS PRINCIPLE:

You Are Connected to Everything and Everyone Else in the Universe

"I am because we are."

— TENET OF THE SOUTH AFRICAN PHILOSOPHY KNOWN AS UBUNTU

The Premise

In this experiment, you'll prove that you are interconnected with everyone and everything through an "invisible" field of intelligence and energy. In quantum-speak, this lattice of connections is called *nonlocality*.

And even though it's one of the signature concepts of quantum mechanics, nonlocality, along with its cousin entanglement, has incited much head-scratching over the last 300 years, starting with Sir Isaac Newton, who considered what he called "action at a distance" ludicrous (despite the fact that his own theory of gravity had proposed just such a phenomenon). To be brief, nonlocality is when two particles behave synchronously with no intermediary.

But it doesn't make logical sense, right? If you want to move, say, an abandoned shoe in the middle of the floor, you have to touch the shoe or touch a broom that touches the shoe or instruct your five-year-old, the one who left it there, to pick it up, via vibrations through the air to his ear. Things can only affect things that are in the immediate vicinity. There has to be a sequence, a chain of events. We believe that we can only alter things we can touch.

But that's not the case. We've now got a demonstrably more accurate model that proves that one object, without being anywhere near a second object, can influence the second object. Unfortunately, most of us still persist in hanging on to the old "chain-of-events" worldview, even though physicists have demonstrated time and time again that once an atom has been in the proximity of another atom, it will be influenced (or entangled) by that atom no matter how far away it travels. Even Einstein couldn't bring himself to fully embrace this counterintuitive concept. An even weirder conundrum is that once the atoms have interacted, they're entangled forever.

We have even proved that nonlocality and entanglement work on bigger things—like humans. In 1978, Dr. Jacobo Grinberg-Zylberbaum of the National Autonomous University of Mexico (later replicated by London neuropsychiatrist Peter Fenwick) hooked two test subjects to electroencephalographs in isolated rooms. The brainwave pattern produced by a series of strobe lights in one of the subject's eyes appeared identically on the other test subject's EEG even though he was nowhere near the same flashes.

Though nonlocality doesn't make sense to our Newtonian brains, we can still use it to our advantage. Like your computer that is hooked up via the Internet to an infinite amount of information, you—by virtue of being a human being—are hooked up to everyone else in the world.

Sometimes, when I want to communicate to someone in another part of the world, I whisper my message to the giant oak tree in my front yard. Needless to say, trees, like the dogs in *101 Dalmatians,* are interconnected, and the oak can easily send messages to a palm tree in a friend's yard in California through the concept of nonlocality.

In this experiment, you're going to use nonlocality to send a message to someone from a distance, someone you will not see or talk to.

That Synching Feeling

"It is all about love and how we all are connected."

— MARK WAHLBERG, AMERICAN ACTOR

When my daughter was in junior high school, she began answering every question with the same reply—222. If someone asked what time it was, she'd say 2:22. Even when it was 5:43. If someone wondered how much it costs for a lunchroom carton of milk, again she'd answer with $2.22. Her friends got a big kick out of it and started calling her at exactly 2:22 every afternoon. She even started a Facebook fan page called "The Amazingly Awesomeness of 222." As I said, she was in junior high. That same summer, we took two trips. On both of these trips, with no input or planning on my part, we ended up staying in room 222 of our hotels—one in Seattle after we missed our connection to Juneau; and the other in London's Langham Hotel, located across from the BBC headquarters.

Swiss psychiatrist Carl Jung called events like these *synchronicity:* "the simultaneous occurrence of two meaningful but not causally connected events." Some people view coincidences like these as amusing anomalies spit out by the random event generator, arguing that it's only inevitable that eventually events from Column A will match up with those from Column B.

In this experiment, you're going to permit yourself to suppose that synchronistic events are not the result of the law of averages or outright delusion, but rather valid products of nonlocality and entanglement.

In fact, in his book *Prometheus Rising,* Robert Anton Wilson claims that even "contemplating these issues usually triggers Jungian synchronicities. See how long after reading this chapter you encounter an amazing coincidence." If you have any great stories, by all means, send them to me via my website: **www.pamgrout.com.**

As Wilson loved to point out, the fabric of the universe doesn't play by human rules. In fact, let's let him explain the theorem of nonlocality put forth in the 1960s by theorist John S. Bell. It was Bell's now-famous theorem that led to actual experiments that conclusively proved the non-local quantum nature of the world:

> Bell's Theorem is highly technical, but in ordinary language it amounts to . . . this: There are no isolated systems; every particle in the universe is in "instantaneous" (faster-than-light) communication with every

other particle. The Whole *System,* even the parts that are separated by cosmic distances, functions as a *Whole System.*

After this experiment, you'll discover that synchronicity, a phenomenon people regularly shrug off with a "Wow! What a weird coincidence," is nothing but experimental proof of the interconnectedness of all things.

Everything That Doesn't Look Like Love Is Smoke and Mirrors

"We can slice and dice it anyway we like, but we cannot justify turning our face away from this evidence."

— LARRY DOSSEY, M.D., AMERICAN PHYSICIAN AND AUTHOR

In 1972, at the annual convention of the American Association for the Advancement of Science, a meteorologist named Edward Lorenz introduced a brand-new term into the American vernacular. The *butterfly effect* was his observation that an event as seemingly insignificant as the flapping of a butterfly's wings in Brazil could set off a hurricane in Texas. In other words, small, almost imperceptible things can have large and momentous consequences.

The cool thing about this experiment is that you can use it to draw love into your life. You can use it to brighten the world. When you generate uplifting thoughts about someone, it contributes favorably to his or her energy. Conversely, when you judge others, even if you keep it to yourself, you affect their energy and weigh down the quality of your interactions. You can literally uplift your world by lasering love, blessings, peace, and other high-frequency emotions to the people in your life.

As it says in *A Course of Miracles*, "You are being blessed by every beneficent thought of any of your brothers anywhere."

There's a story about a protester who was outside the Military School of America, taking a silent stand against the policies of the United State and its bullying behavior. Someone asked him, "What makes you think holding that little candle is going to have any effect on these governments? They've been doing what they do for decades now."

He replied, "I'm not worried about changing them. I don't want my country to change *me*."

Your thoughts about other people change *you*.

Is it really possible in this us-versus-them world that we, as this energy principle states, are really one?

Well, to be blunt—yeah. We're all in this together. And every time we judge or think anything less than charitable about anyone, we crucify ourselves. We inflict self-pain.

Our differences, as huge as we make them out to be, are superficial and meaningless. And it's time we let them go.

When you meet anyone, remember that it is a holy encounter. As you see him you will see yourself. As you treat him you will treat yourself. As you think of him you will think of yourself.

You can change your relationship with anyone by simply sending them good thoughts.

Anecdotal Evidence

"All we want, whether we are honeybees, ponderosa pines, coyotes, human beings, or stars, is to love and be loved, to be accepted, cherished and celebrated simply for being who we are. Is that so very difficult?"

— DERRICK JENSEN, AMERICAN AUTHOR AND ENVIRONMENTAL ACTIVIST

My friend, whom I'll call Ginger because that is not her name, had a rocky relationship with her mother for years. Finally, she decided that every night before falling asleep she would send her mom blessings. Her mom, of course, had no idea she was doing this. To this day, Ginger has never told her mother that for about six months, she spent a few minutes each evening envisioning her getting all the things she ever wanted and seeing herself being happy about it.

"I honestly don't know how it happened, but our relationship changed. Now, we're the best of friends," Ginger says.

More Anecdotal Evidence

*"Explore your own higher latitudes. Be a
Columbus to whole new continents within you,
opening new channels, not of trade, but of thought.*

— HENRY DAVID THOREAU, AMERICAN WRITER AND PHILOSOPHER

Best-selling author Martha Beck was once like most of us: friendly enough, trusting enough, but not about to go overboard. After all, she was a scientist, a Harvard-pedigreed sociologist who needed facts to form any kind of conclusion. And the conclusion she came to, the same one most all of us come to on planet Earth, is that people are okay, but you don't want to get too involved. Especially not if you're at Harvard and trying to get your second graduate degree. Probably best to keep people at arm's length.

As she describes it in her wonderful book *Expecting Adam*, "We go around like Queen Elizabeth, bless her heart, clutching our dowdy little accessories, avoiding the slightest hint of impropriety, never showing our real feelings or touching anyone else except through glove leather."

But life pulled a fast one on Martha Beck. It gave her a son with Down syndrome (Adam) who taught her that everything she thought she understood about the world is a big ruse. Especially the part about not trusting other people. When she was pregnant with Adam, her husband, also a Harvard graduate student, traveled to Asia a lot, and she was left at home to cope with her demanding studies, their two-year-old, and a pregnancy that was not going well. Fires, potential miscarriages, and ongoing pregnancy ailments drove her to wit's end.

As she says, "I felt like a load of gravel had been dumped on me."

Every time she was about to snap, an angel (and I don't mean metaphorically) or an acquaintance she barely knew would show up with kind words, groceries, or some other assistance. Keep in mind that this is a woman who had to be on the edge of desperation for anything this woo-woo to get through. She had long ago eschewed any notion of God and was sworn by education to follow "the good old Baconian logic of refusing to believe anything until it was proven true."

Nonetheless, a woman she barely knew showed up on her doorstep with groceries one morning when she was about to pass out, an unseen force appeared out of nowhere to guide her and her daughter through her smoke-filled apartment before it burned to the ground, and she was able to see and talk to her husband even though he was in Hong Kong and she was in Boston. And, no, I don't mean by telephone.

What she came to realize is: "Against all odds, despite everything that works against it on this unpleasant, uncomfortable planet, mothering is here in abundance. You can always find it, if you're smart enough and know where to look." Even if you aren't smart enough, it tends to show up—especially if you really need it.

Says Beck: "I have to jettison every sorrow, every terror, every misconception, every lie that stands between my conscious mind and what I know in my heart to be true. . . . I have expanded my reality from a string of solid facts, as narrow, strong, and cold as a razor's edge, to a wild chaos of possibility."

The Method

"What now appear as the paradoxes of quantum theory will seem just as common sense to our children's children."

— STEPHEN HAWKING, BRITISH THEORETICAL PHYSICIST

In this experiment you're going to send a message to someone you know using the concept of nonlocality. According to Laura Day, author of *Practical Intuition*, it's as easy as sending an e-mail.

The good thing about this experiment is you don't even have to leave your easy chair. The majority of your interactions with other humans occur in the nonphysical realm. All those thoughts you think you're privately keeping to yourself? They're not really private. Since we're all connected, you might as well be bellowing them over an intercom. Subtly, everyone is getting the message anyway.

We're all connected to this huge data bank, and we constantly exchange energy with everyone in our circle of influence, and in smaller ways, with every other being on the planet.

Forget therapy. You can save all kinds of cash by simply changing the dialogue within your own mind.

But be careful what you ask for. Sondra Ray, co-founder of Loving Relationship Training and a former teacher of mine, tells a funny story about communicating through the unseen energy data bank. She went to Leonard Orr, another one of my teachers, to find out why she kept wrecking her car. He told her to make a different intention in the form of an affirmation. She scoffed and said, "You mean to tell me that with nothing but an intention I could even get men to call me on the telephone?"

"Of course," he said. "Try it."

She began sending this intention out into the FP: *I now receive an abundant inflow of calls from men.* Within four days, every single one of her old lovers called, some of whom she hadn't seen in months, some for years.

"Incredible as it sounds," she says, "I began to receive calls during the night, wrong numbers from men I didn't even know." Needless to say, she changed that intention to one that worked.

Here are the steps:

1. Choose your target. While it's certainly possible to send a message to practically anyone, I suggest choosing someone you've already met. Bruce Rosenblum, professor of physics at the University of California–Santa Cruz, claims that once you've met someone and shaken that person's hand, you are forever entangled.

2. Choose what kind of action or response you want. The more specific you can get, the better. Be very clear about your agenda. For my most recent experiment, I sent a message

to my partner Jim: "Bring home a loaf of bread."

3. Place your target in front of your mind's eye.
4. "Be" with your target by embodying and experiencing your connection. Words are often an ineffective way to get a message across. Engage all your senses. And believe in your message.

To make it more effective and to add a little fun, shower your target with good thoughts. Send them incomparable blessings. Think about them winning the lottery, getting a date with Channing Tatum, winning a trip around the world.

Lab Report Sheet

The Principle: The 101 Dalmatians Principle

The Theory: You are connected to everything and everyone else in the universe.

The Question: Can I send a message to someone without being in that person's presence?

The Hypothesis: If during the next two days, I telepathically send a specific message to a specific person, I will get evidence that he or she received it.

Time Required: 48 hours

The Approach: Okay, FP, I'm hearing the melody from *The Twilight Zone* playing in the background, but I'm willing to suspend judgment just this once to see if this might be one of those mysterious aspects of quantum physics. What say you?

Today's Date: _____ **Time:** _____

Research Notes: _____

_____

∷ ∷ ∷

"That is at bottom the only courage that is demanded of us: to have courage for the most strange, the most singular and the most inexplicable that we may encounter."

— Rainer Maria Rilke, Bohemian-Austrian poet

THE FISH AND LOAVES PRINCIPLE

The Universe Is Limitless, Abundant, and Strangely Accommodating

"Most people come to know only one corner of their room, one spot near the window, one narrow strip on which they keep walking back and forth."
— RAINER MARIA RILKE, BOHEMIAN-AUSTRIAN POET

The Premise

This experiment will dispel the myth that life sucks and then you die. Most of us, whether we admit it or not, believe life is hard. We believe there's only so much to go around—whether we're talking money, time, or popcorn at the multiplex cinema. Even people with Maseratis in their garage spend way too much time figuring out how to get more.

Why? Because they mistakenly believe there's not enough. Even billionaires, even people with an overabundance of resources, live under the oppressive spell of "there's not enough."

A friend of mine was interviewing the wealthy owner of a successful business whose company was launching a new product. Noticing the rabid dollar signs in his eyes, she asked him if there was a profit margin, a success index, a dollar amount of some kind that he would consider "enough." The business owner stopped for a moment, sighed, and gave this reply: "Man, you just don't get it. There is never enough."

It's like the game musical chairs. Everyone's worried that when the music stops, they'll be the one without a place to sit.

We're rich beyond measure, but we feel strapped, scared, and always on guard. Sure, we call ourselves an abundant society, but in many ways it's nothing but an illusion, a ruse, thanks to the ever-present "there's not enough" mantra. We're too busy playing musical chairs, running faster and faster around that illusory circle of shrinking chairs. Contrary to everything you know, the Fish and Loaves principle proposes that there is a natural law of abundance and that everything's okay—you can relax.

When Jesus "prayed" to multiply the fish and loaves, he didn't fret over how this might come about. He simply put all his thoughts into one laser-like formation—namely, that abundance and plenty were his divine right. Likewise, for the duration of this experiment, you're going to set aside your normal thinking patterns and allow them to be superseded by the remote possibility that there might be enough. For everyone.

Something Is Wrong with This Picture

"If you think there's a bogeyman, turn on the light."

— DOROTHY THOMPSON, AMERICAN JOURNALIST AND BROADCASTER

Scarcity and lack is our default setting, the unquestioned conditioning that defines our lives. The belief that "there's not enough" starts first thing every morning when the alarm clock rings: "Ah, shit, I didn't get enough z's."

Before we even sit up, before we even squeeze our feet into our bunny slippers, we're already bemoaning lack. When we finally do get up, it's "Now I don't have enough time to get ready."

And from there it goes downhill.

We spend large chunks of our energy worrying and complaining about not getting enough. We don't have enough time. We don't get enough exercise or fiber or vitamin E. Our paychecks aren't big enough. Our weekends aren't long enough. We, poor things, are not thin enough, smart enough, or educated enough.

It never even occurs to us to examine whether this "not enough" mantra is true. It's so profoundly ingrained that it shapes our deepest sense of who we are. Being deficient has become the lens through which we experience every facet of life.

It's why we take jobs that don't satisfy us. It's why we stay in unfulfilling relationships. It's why we keep going back to the buffet line long after our appetites have been filled. It's why we've created systems and institutions to control access to resources (oil, anyone?) that we perceive as valuable and limited. If we weren't so worried about not having enough, we could relax and use the resources we do have to develop alternative sources of energy, like the sun or the wind—energy, I hasten to point out, that will never run out.

This "not enough" fiction drives us to do things we're not proud of, things that compromise our highest ideals, things that lay waste to the natural world, things that separate us from our highest selves. And once we define ourselves as deficient, all our energy gets sucked into making sure we're not the one being left out, not the one losing ground to the "other guy."

But here's the deal. It's all a big, fat, unfortunate lie. There is enough—for everyone. We live in a big, bounteous universe, and if we can just get over this unfounded fear of not enough, we can stop hoarding resources (c'mon, who really needs 89 pairs of shoes?) and free up our energy to make sure all of us get what we need.

The Chumash Native Americans, who lived for thousands of years on the central coast of California, enjoyed what I would call rich and prosperous lives. They lived in small, close-knit villages and used the natural resources around them to make canoes, arrows, and medicines. They regularly dined on more than 150 kinds of seafood, honeydew melons, and pine nuts. They made fur blankets, soapstone pots decorated with shells, and extraordinary baskets, so tightly woven they could hold water. Almost every day the Chumash played games, danced, sang lullabies to their children, and enjoyed a cleansing sweat in the village 'apa'yik.

Nowadays, we call that type of lifestyle "subsistence." We look down upon it as a hardscrabble existence. But what I'd like to suggest is that the Chumash, unlike us, lived in an economy of abundance. To the Chumash, there was always enough. Not too much. Not too little. Enough. Most important, there was enough time for things that matter—relationships, delicious food, art, games, and rest.

Right now, with the resources already at your disposal (you don't have to get a new job or find a new relationship or even start a time-consuming new yoga practice), you can begin to recognize and lead a rich and meaningful life. And the best part is, you can quit working so damned hard. Take it easy for a change.

"Bliss" Happens

"What if this powerful force was used to uplift people rather than keep them trapped in the corporate and religious food chain?"

— MARK VICENTE, DIRECTOR OF *WHAT THE BLEEP DO WE KNOW!?*

The bottom line is, we have no conception of the limits we have placed on our perception. If we really knew the extent to which we have denied the world's loveliness, we would be shocked.

Our confusion is so profound that we cannot even conceive of the world without sacrifice. But here's the thing: The world contains no sacrifice except what we laid upon it.

It's worth pausing for a moment to consider just how deluded we've become.

⊞ ⊞ ⊞

A few days after Eckhart Tolle's 29th birthday, he suffered an intense anxiety attack. He had suicidal thoughts.

His life so far had basically sucked. On this particular night, he kept saying to himself, over and over again, "I cannot live with myself any longer." Suddenly, he says, "I could feel myself being sucked into a void."

When he "woke up," all he could experience was love, a state of deep, uninterrupted peace and bliss.

His intense emotional pain forced his consciousness to withdraw from all the limits he had placed on it. The withdrawal was so complete that his deluded self, his unhappy and deeply fearful self, immediately collapsed like an inflatable toy with the plug removed.

He spent almost two years doing nothing but sitting on park benches in a state of intense joy.

Or consider Byron Katie. This California Realtor was in the middle of an ordinary life—two marriages, three kids, a successful career—when she went into a deep depression. She checked herself into a halfway house for women with eating disorders, not because she had an eating disorder but because it was the only facility her insurance company would cover. One night, while lying on the floor in the attic ("I felt too unworthy to sleep in a bed," she says), she suddenly woke up without any of life's normal preconceived notions of sacrifice.

"All the thoughts that had been troubling me, my whole world, *the* whole world, was gone. . . . Everything was unrecognizable. . . . Laughter welled up from the depths and just poured out. . . . [I] was intoxicated with joy," she says in her book *A Thousand Names for Joy.*

She went home and sat by the window, staring out in complete bliss for days on end.

"It was like freedom had woken up inside me," she says.

Colonel Mustard, in the Conservatory, with the Wrench

"Common sense is the collection of prejudices acquired by age eighteen."

— ALBERT EINSTEIN, GERMAN THEORETICAL PHYSICIST

I was playing the board game *Clue* with a couple of my daughter's friends. We passed out the detective notebooks and placed the rope, the lead pipe, and the other miniature weapons in the miniature mansion's miniature rooms.

I said to Kylie, who was playing Professor Plum, "Why don't you go first?"

The girls looked at me as if I'd just asked them to take a shower in the boys' locker room.

"Mom!"

"Miss Grout!" they loudly protested.

"What? What did I say?"

"Everybody knows Miss Scarlet always goes first."

Likewise, they explained that in order to make an accusation, you have to be in the room where you think the murder took place, and if you want to take a secret passageway, you can only do it between the parlor and the kitchen or the library and the conservatory.

"Who says?" I asked.

"The rules. It says so right here." One of them thrust the neatly printed rule sheet in my face.

These "engraved-in-stone rules" remind me of how we *"play life."* Somebody decided that this is how the world "works," and because we all agreed to see it that way, we made it "reality."

Turns out, we've all been had. Nearly all the concepts and judgments we take for granted are gross distortions of things as they really are. Everything we think is "real" is simply a reflection of the "*Clue* rules" we all agreed upon. The world we think we see is merely the projection of our own individual "*Clue* rules."

Maybe it's time to take those *Clue* rules, cut them up, and use them as confetti. Until we do, until we finally get it that we are "wholly loved, wholly lovable, and wholly loving," we will continue to feel empty, question our purpose, and wonder why we're here.

That's why we need to ask for a whole new lens for looking at the world.

Anecdotal Evidence

"Being gloomy is easier than being cheerful. Anybody can say 'I've got cancer' and get a rise out of a crowd. But how many of us can do five minutes of good stand-up comedy?"

— P.J. O'ROURKE, FORMER *ROLLING STONE* CORRESPONDENT

Caryn Johnson always knew she wanted to be an actor. In fact, she says her first coherent thought as a young child was, *Man, I'd love to act.*

Even though she grew up in the New York projects, theater and what she called "pretending to be somebody else" was a big part of her life. This was back in the days when Joe Papp brought free Shakespeare to her neighborhood in Chelsea. She also watched lots of movies with her brother, Clyde, and her mom, Emma, who raised the two kids on a single salary.

"When I saw Carole Lombard coming down some stairs in a long satin thing, I thought, I can do that," she says. "I wanted to come down those stairs and say those words and live that life. You could be anything, up there in the movies.

You could fly. You could meet alien life-forms. You could be a queen. You could sleep in a great big bed, with satin sheets, in your own room."

By the time she was eight, she was acting for the Hudson Guild Community Center, a children's day care/theater/arts program near her neighborhood.

Her life took a detour in high school when her dyslexia caused her to get mistakenly classified as "slow, possibly retarded." She dropped out of school, became a junkie, and forgot all about her acting dream. By the time she was 19, she was a single mom herself.

The good news is she *did* kick the drugs. In fact, her daughter's father was the drug counselor who helped her get off the junk. But the bad news is, he wasn't cut out to be a father. He left a few months after their daughter Alexandrea was born.

Caryn was a high school dropout with no skills. In fact, the only thing she knew how to do was take care of kids. She took a job as a nanny and moved to Lubbock, Texas, with the friend who hired her. Eventually, the friend moved to San Diego, and Caryn and her daughter gladly followed.

When the relationship went south, she found herself stuck in California with no money and no skills. She didn't even know how to drive, a major hindrance in freeway-happy California.

"I had no high school diploma," she says. "All I had was me and my kid."

Oh yeah, and that *Man, I'd love to act* dream. During the day, she learned to lay bricks and went to cosmetology school. At night, she played around with an experimental theater troupe. For a while she did hair and makeup for a funeral home, supplementing her income with a welfare check, "worrying about how to get my kid more than one pair of shoes, or how to make $165 worth of groceries last for a month."

Through it all, she continued to believe that "anything is possible." She continued to believe that she could be like Carole Lombard, floating down the stairs in satin.

"Acting is the one thing I always knew I could do," she says.

Her unwavering belief finally unlocked the door. In 1983, famed Hollywood director Mike Nichols happened to catch her performance in an experimental troupe in Berkeley, the Black Street Hawkeyes. He was so blown away by the characters she played that he signed her immediately for a one-woman performance, *The Spook Show,* on Broadway. Steven Spielberg caught that show and cast her as Celie in *The Color Purple.* By then, she'd changed her name to Whoopi Goldberg.

"I can do anything. I can be anything. No one ever told me I couldn't. No one ever expressed this idea that I was limited to any one thing, and so I think in terms of what's possible, not impossible," Whoopi said in her autobiography, *Book.*

"I knew I could never turn water into wine or make cats speak French. But I also learned that if you come to a thing with no preconceived notions of what that thing is, the whole world can be your canvas.

"Just dream it and you can make it so. I believe I belong wherever I want to be, in whatever situation or context I place myself. I believed a little girl could rise from a single-parent household in the Manhattan projects, start a single-parent household of her own, struggle though seven years of welfare and odd jobs and still wind up making movies.

"So, yeah, I think anything is possible. I know it because I have lived it. I know it because I have seen it. I have witnessed things that ancients have called miracles, but they are not miracles. They are the products of someone's dream. As human beings, we are capable of creating a paradise, and making each other's lives better by our own hands. Yes, yes, yes—this is possible.

"If something hasn't happened, it's not because it can't happen, or won't: it just hasn't happened yet."

More Anecdotal Evidence

"Harnessing the power of your mind can be more effective than the drugs you have been programmed to believe you need."

— BRUCE LIPTON, PH.D., AMERICAN CELL BIOLOGIST

For years, Myrtle Fillmore's life revolved around her cabinet full of medicine. Not only did the eventual co-founder of Unity Church suffer from tuberculosis, which caused her to spit up blood and run a near-constant fever, but she also had aggravated malaria. One day, she attended a lecture by New Thought teacher Dr. E. B. Weeks, who made the outrageous claim that God, who was all-good, would never wish disease on anyone. Furthermore, he said, if she aligned herself with this all-good spirit, she would discover her true self—which could only be healthy.

Over and over, Myrtle began affirming, "I am a child of God and therefore do not inherit sickness." She refused to "judge according to appearance" and praised the vital energy of God within every cell of her body. Little by little, Myrtle began to get better. Within two years, there was no sign of her old illnesses.

Myrtle's husband, Charles, witnessed the remarkable healing of his wife and decided to try the same affirmations. He, too, was considered disabled. Thanks to a boyhood skating accident and a subsequent series of operations, his hip socket was badly damaged and one of his legs had stopped growing. He wore a steel extension to make his legs even. He figured the best he could do was learn to live with the chronic pain.

Like Myrtle, Charles Fillmore began to affirm that there is an all-good, all-powerful energy force. Not only was he completely cured of pain within a year, but his shortened leg caught up with the other one. The universe took care of him.

The Method

"Reality is merely an illusion, albeit a persistent one."

—ALBERT EINSTEIN, GERMAN THEORETICAL PHYSICIST

This experiment will prove what Sally Field finally figured out when she won the Oscar for *Places in the Heart:* "You like me, you really like me." It will prove how sublime our world truly is.

For the next 48 hours, we're going to keep track of goodness and beauty.

The record of history, of course, is written in blood—in wars, treachery, and competition. But as paleontologist Stephen Jay Gould said, "The fossil record shows long, uninterrupted periods of biological stability."

In fact, it's a structural paradox that one violent act so distracts us from the 10,000 acts of kindness. Human courtesy, kindness, and beauty, he claimed, are the norm.

He called it our duty, our holy responsibility, to record and honor the victorious weight of all the innumerable little kindnesses that are all too often unnoted and invisible.

Keep a journal on hand for the next two days, and list these kindnesses. Here are some examples of what you might enumerate:

- "My wife gave me a kiss before I left for my doctor's appointment."

- "The receptionist and I compared pictures of her new baby and my new grandson."

- "When I entered my office with an armload of books, a stranger held the door for me."

- "The man at the lunch counter smiled and said, 'Wassup?'"

- "Students in the overcrowded lunchroom graciously shared a table."

- "My e-mail misbehaved, and a colleague helped me sort it out."

- "A colleague in another state responded to my testy message with grace and goodwill."

Lab Report Sheet

The Principle: The Fish and Loaves Principle

The Theory: The universe is limitless, abundant, and strangely accommodating.

The Question: Is my focus on the negative keeping me from seeing reality?

The Hypothesis: If I change my outlook and make a concerted effort to look for goodness, beauty, and abundance, it will show up in spades.

Time Required: 48 hours

Today's Date: _____ **Time:** _____

Number of kind, beautiful, good things: _____

The Approach: I've heard the old adage "What you appreciate appreciates." So I guess I'll give it a whirl. Who knows? Maybe expressing gratitude is more that just some mumbo-jumbo Pollyanna/Oprah thing. Willie Nelson, after all, said that when he started counting his blessings, his whole life turned around. Like Willie, I'm ready to bet on the probability of peace, bliss, and joy. Consequently, I will actively seek goodness with a vengeance.

Research Notes: _____

_____

:: :: ::

"We have more possibilities
available in each moment than we realize."

— THICH NHAT HANH, BUDDHIST MONK AND PEACE ACTIVIST

AFTERWORD

Lift Each Other Up

*"It is good to come together for the
purpose of co-creating."*
— ABRAHAM-HICKS

High fives! Fist bumps! You made it through the book, and hopefully through the nine experiments. You've bravely cast your hat into the ring. That means the hardest part is over. But if you quit now, you miss the best part of the whole adventure. This is where the payback begins.

What I'd like to suggest is that you form a group in your hometown or home church or even Home Depot (although don't tell them I sent you) with other readers of *E-Squared*.

Even though the FP is always with us, always guiding us, sometimes it helps to have real human bodies to remind us. And heaven knows, we could use the company.

That's why it's vital to find partners in crime, other spiritual warriors who are willing to listen, to cheer, and to remind you just why you're doing this. As Abraham-Hicks likes to say, "When you get tuned in to the energy that creates worlds, the Universe will match you with others with similar vibrations."

It's almost like a cosmic dating service. These "teammates" will enter your vibrational sphere (like attracts like), and together, you'll be able to "square" the energy until it explodes exponentially into a juicy new world and delicious new way of being. Number one guideline? Play and have fun. That is and always will be the ultimate energy generator.

Create a protective circle so each of you will feel safe and valued. It doesn't require a four-hour commitment. Maybe you'll do it over the phone. But it's important to enlist others with whom you can share the results of your experiments—others who are also experimenting.

Share stories. Inspire one another. Make up new experiments. My group proposes a different experiment each week. These can be anything from calming the energy in a busy, hectic room (works like a charm; you just radiate peace and stillness and watch how it changes the energy in, for example, a restaurant or a highly charged meeting) to changing the tenor of a relationship in which you hold automatic judgments and conclusions. My group has a ball reporting back about our successes and about the times we failed to move out of "old-school" conditioning—both powerful lesson plans.

In these circles, it's imperative to talk about and focus on life the way you want it to be, not about how it may appear. Instead of asking "What's wrong?"—probably the most repeated question in the entire English language—focus on "What's right?" That's the only question that really means anything. The answer is the new, more joyful story you're endeavoring to create. During every get-together, share examples of how your life is improving and growing.

And as always, appreciate, embellish, affirm, and dream as you keep these three things in mind:

1. You are awesome. Whether you realize it or not, you are a tremendously powerful energetic being. Currents of possibilities run deep through your bones.

2. The great field of potentiality is unlimited. Absolutely anything is possible. All it takes is the willingness to open your mind, surrender "old-school" conditioning, and continue to expand into more joyful, freer, bigger ideas.

3. We're all in this together. If we take care of one another and go the extra mile to appreciate and play together, we all gain— each one of us is lifted up. Sure, we could walk alone to the finish line. But the real joy comes from tackling the journey together, from raising our voices in one mighty, unified *wahoo!*

BOOK-CLUB DISCUSSION QUESTIONS

1. Pick an experiment and have the group work with it. What were the results? Try a different experiment each week, and see what happens.

2. Do you really believe that there is an invisible force field or field of infinite possibilities (FP)? What are some of your own beliefs? Do you feel that you have a strong faith, or are you more skeptical?

3. In the book Pam says that she appointed God as the CEO of her career. How hard is it for you to let go of the wheel and have some faith in a force in the universe that is working in your favor?

4. This book takes the premise of the popular 2006 book and movie *The Secret* a little further by giving us exercises to do that *prove* the existence of a power or force greater than

ourselves. Do you think that this energy has an intelligence?

5. We draw from the field what we are looking for. Do you find yourself often expecting the worst? How do you deal with this?

6. Pam says in the book, "Don't give any airtime to the reality from which you're trying to escape. Tune in only to your intent" (page 12). Do you find yourself focusing more on what you *don't* want than what you *do* want? What do you do to try to shift this?

7. What do you think of this statement: "Misery loves company"? When you start to pay attention, do you notice more and more people focusing on the negative or what's wrong with their lives?

8. Pam says that training your brain is like housebreaking a puppy. If you keep pushing yourself to be aware of your thoughts over and over, it will become a habit. Do you have a thought habit you would like to change?

9. In Experiment #1 Pam asks us our impressions of God and what we think that is. Has your notion of God changed from when you were a kid? What were some of your ideas back then?

ACKNOWLEDGMENTS

I've heard it takes a village to raise a child. Well, it also takes one to produce a book.

The "village people" for *E-Squared* includes, but is not limited to:

All the coolios at Hay House: Alex Freemon, Shannon Littrell, Christy Salinas, Pam Homan, and Stacey Smith, who went to bat for me from the beginning. Thank you, Stacey! And thank you, Christy, for expediting this amazing cover.

Alex, I balked when I first saw all your comments and corrections, but now I bow to your insight. You were an answer to a prayer.

Jim Dick, who is one of the top three most patient people on the planet; Kitty Shea; Joyce Barrett; Betty Shaffer; the Fusion Sisters; my fellow Wednesday-morning Spiritual Entrepreneurs; my Vortex group; and, of course, Taz.

ABOUT THE AUTHOR

Pam Grout is the author of 16 books, three plays, a television series, and two iPhone apps. She writes for *People* magazine, **CNNgo.com**, *The Huffington Post,* and her travel blog, **www.georgeclooneyslepthere.com**. Find out more about Pam and her out-of-the-box take on life at her sometimes-updated website: **www.pamgrout.com**.

We hope you enjoyed this Hay House Insights book. If you'd like to receive our online catalog featuring additional information on Hay House books and products, or if you'd like to find out more about the Hay Foundation, please contact:

INSIGHTS

Hay House, Inc., P.O. Box 5100, Carlsbad, CA 92018-5100
(760) 431-7695 or (800) 654-5126
(760) 431-6948 (fax) or (800) 650-5115 (fax)
www.hayhouse.com® • www.hayfoundation.org

⊞ ⊞ ⊞

Published and distributed in Australia by: Hay House Australia Pty. Ltd.,
18/36 Ralph St., Alexandria NSW 2015 • *Phone:* 612-9669-4299
Fax: 612-9669-4144 • www.hayhouse.com.au

Published and distributed in the United Kingdom by: Hay House UK, Ltd.,
Astley House, 33 Notting Hill Gate, London W11 3JQ • *Phone:* 44-20-3675-2450 • *Fax:* 44-20-3675-2451 • www.hayhouse.co.uk

Published and distributed in the Republic of South Africa by:
Hay House SA (Pty), Ltd., P.O. Box 990, Witkoppen 2068
Phone/Fax: 27-11-467-8904 • www.hayhouse.co.za

Published in India by: Hay House Publishers India, Muskaan Complex,
Plot No. 3, B-2, Vasant Kunj, New Delhi 110 070
Phone: 91-11-4176-1620 • *Fax:* 91-11-4176-1630 • www.hayhouse.co.in

Distributed in Canada by: Raincoast Books, 2440 Viking Way, Richmond,
B.C. V6V 1N2 • *Phone:* 1-800-663-5714 • *Fax:* 1-800-565-3770
www.raincoast.com

⊞ ⊞ ⊞

Take Your Soul on a Vacation

Visit **www.HealYourLife.com®** to regroup, recharge, and reconnect with your own magnificence. Featuring blogs, mind-body-spirit news, and life-changing wisdom from Louise Hay and friends.

Visit **www.HealYourLife.com** today!